Pawns
or
Potentates

Pawns or Potentates

The Reality
of America's
Corporate Boards

Jay W. Lorsch
with
Elizabeth MacIver

Harvard Business School Press
Boston, Massachusetts

05 04 03   10 9 8 7

The paper used in this publication meets the
requirements of the American National Standard for
Permanence of Paper for Printed Library Materials Z39.49-1984.

Library of Congress Cataloging-in-Publication Data

Lorsch, Jay William.
    Pawns or potentates : the reality of America's corporate boards /
Jay W. Lorsch with Elizabeth MacIver.
      p. cm.
    Includes bibliographical references.
    ISBN 0-87584-216-X (alk. paper)
    1. Directors of corporations—United States. 2. Directors of
corporations—Europe. I. MacIver, Elizabeth, 1964- . II. Title.
HD2745.L56 1989
658.4'22'0973—dc20   89-20038
                                      CIP

**In memory of
Hans R. Lorsch**

Contents

Preface

This book and the study that led to it began in 1986, took over three years, and involved the cooperation of more than 1,100 people, of whom more than 900 are unknown to us by name because they are outside directors of the Standard & Poor's 400 companies, who completed our questionnaire. What we do know is that they are representative of the population from which they self-selected in age, primary occupation, number of directorships held, and size of the companies on whose boards they sit. We also know that the response rate of 32% is very high for a mail questionnaire.

A group of 100 directors was randomly selected to be interviewed. Of these we were able to talk with about 80. Most of the interviews lasted an hour or more and were conducted by MacIver throughout the United States and in several European countries. Additionally, we met with a half-dozen British CEOs and officials of PRONED, an organization that encourages British companies to select a higher proportion of nonexecutive directors to their boards.

We also interviewed about 35 directors and other corporate officers in connection with the book's four cases on boards and crisis. MacIver also conducted most of these interviews, supervised the collection and analysis of the questionnaire data, and prepared the cases. To all these directors and company officers who gave us their time and shared their thoughts and recollections, we are extremely grateful. Their help has enabled us to complete the most comprehensive study of American corporate governance ever undertaken.

Another group who gave us time were our colleagues at the Harvard Business School. About ten people, who are themselves outside directors of public companies, were the guinea pigs upon whom we tested our questionnaire. Others, including Joseph Auerbach, Chris Argyris, E. Raymond Corey,

Gordon Donaldson, Paul Lawrence, and Walter Salmon, read an early draft of this book. Their comments and suggestions were all extremely helpful. While indebted to them all, we especially want to recognize the help of Chris Argyris, who contributed to our ideas about group norms in the boardroom and the problem of "undiscussability," and that of Joe Auerbach, now "of counsel" to Sullivan & Worcester, who taught us the rudiments of the legal perspective. We are also grateful to Joseph Flom of Skadden, Arps, Slate, Meagher & Flom, to Leo Herzel of Mayer, Brown & Platt, to Joseph Hinsey of the Harvard Business School, and to James Melican, General Counsel of International Paper Company, for contributing to our further understanding of the legal perspective.

We also want to acknowledge the contribution of Standard & Poor's, which provided the original data base about directors, and of *Directorship* publication, which provided information from its data base. We are also grateful to the Dayton-Hudson Corporation for permission to use its diagram describing directors' duties.

Many others helped make our ideas clearer, especially Patricia Welbourn, who used her considerable literary talents to make this book as readable as possible. Richard Luecke, our editor at the Harvard Business School Press, and Natalie Greenberg, Production Editor of the Press, made numerous contributions. Annmarie Fennelly kept us organized in the data-gathering stage, and Julie Leith managed the numerous drafts through the hardworking word-processing staff. All of them may have read much more about corporate governance than they ever wanted to.

Finally, we must thank Dean John McArthur and the Division of Research at the school for their financial support and personal encouragement.

While all of these individuals made our study possible, we, of course, are responsible for any errors of commission or omission.

Boston, Massachusetts   Jay W. Lorsch
May 1989   Elizabeth MacIver

Pawns
or
Potentates

Chapter 1

Governance Legalities and Realities

Boardroom—the word alone conjures up visions of power, wealth, and privilege in the minds of most Americans. Almost every publicly owned corporation in America has a boardroom, impressively designed and furnished in a fashion that does nothing to undermine the popular view. The boardroom's core, the symbol of its power, is a massive, highly polished table around which the directors are presumed to make the decisions that govern the corporation and affect the wealth of its owners—the shareholders—and the livelihood of its employees.

This symbol of power seems as appropriate to the company's employees, including many of its managers, as it does to the general public who invest their savings, directly or indirectly, through mutual or pension funds in the shares of the companies. This perception of the role and the power of the board of directors meshes, too, with the traditional legal view of corporate governance.

Directors, however, are less sanguine about their power and capacity to govern. While they don't see themselves as pawns of management, as did their predecessors of a decade ago, they acknowledge a number of constraints on their ability to govern in a timely and effective manner. Such constraints include their own available time and knowledge, a lack of consensus about their goals, and the superior power of man-

1

agement, particularly the CEO-chairman.[1] These are the major conclusions of our research into corporate governance in U.S. publicly owned companies, an investigation prompted by the obvious malaise of U.S. business performance over the past decade.

Accusatory fingers have pointed in many directions but, to date, few have questioned the role of those ultimately legally responsible for the health of America's corporations—their boards of directors. Some have blamed top management's shortsightedness and rigidity for the decline of entire industries, such as automobile, consumer electronics, and steel, and for the ills of major companies within these industries.[2] Others have laid the blame on the high wages and lack of productivity of U.S. workers.[3] Still others have diagnosed the problem as a lack of coherent U.S. industrial policy and business-government cooperation like that which is found in Japan and other Pacific-rim countries.[4] While these possibilities and many others may have merit, what is most striking in the debate is the almost universal exclusion from consideration or censure of that major symbol of American corporate power—the board of directors.[5]

In addition, despite directors' close involvement with the wave of unfriendly takeovers and related mergers, the restructurings and leveraged buyouts, few observers have questioned their role in allowing the market value of their companies' equities to become low enough to make the takeover game so attractive to raiders. The resulting changes in the corporate portrait are significant, some might say staggering. Of the

---

1. The two positions are held by the same person in about 80% of U.S. public companies.
2. William J. Abernathy and Robert H. Hayes, "Managing Our Way to Economic Decline," *Harvard Business Review* (July–August 1980), pp. 67–77.
3. Ezra J. Vogel, *Japan as Number One* (Cambridge, Mass.: Harvard University Press, 1976), pp. 131–157.
4. George C. Lodge, *The American Disease* (New York: Alfred A. Knopf, 1984), p. 279.
5. An exception to this statement is by Arch Patton and John C. Baker, "Why Directors Won't Rock the Boat," *Harvard Business Review* (November–December 1987), pp. 10–18. They blame directors for the fact that U.S. companies have not been able to compete in world markets, pointing out that "12 out of 21 leading manufacturing industries in the United States have run to the federal government for protection."

"400" companies listed in *Standard & Poor's* in 1977, 157 had disappeared by 1987. Of that vanished number, 109 had been acquired or had merged, and the rate of such activity has been accelerating. As Fruhan reports, "The dollar value of mergers between 1985 and 1987 exceeded $520 billion—ten times the value of mergers between 1975 and 1977."[6] From 1983 to 1987, he adds, nearly 30% of the market value of U.S. companies evaporated through acquisition or merger.[7]

Another, more subtle change has emerged in the shift of company ownership from individual stockholders to institutions. It is difficult to pinpoint the exact percentage of shares of publicly owned companies held by institutions, but we can state that it's as high as 66% and in the case of some large companies exceeds 70%.[8] Again, understanding how directors deal with this challenge seemed important.

We wanted to learn how current corporate governance practices were contributing to any or all of these changes and challenges, and which difficulties, if any, were inhibiting directors in dealing with events and issues confronting U.S. companies in the past decade. We wanted to know how directors view their role and their responsibility as corporate governors in a changing landscape, how well they feel they are governing, and what are the barriers to more effective governance.

In describing our findings and proposing ideas for improvement, we do not want to convert the management-and-worker bashing of the early 1980s into bashing the board.

6. William E. Fruhan, Jr., "Corporate Raiders! Head 'Em off at Value Gap," *Harvard Business Review* (July–August 1988), p. 63.

7. Ibid., p. 64.

8. Our own analysis of company ownership of the *S&P's* 400 in 1987 indicated institutional ownership of more than 50%. Peter Drucker in "Management and the World's Work," *Harvard Business Review* (September–October 1988), p. 71, and in private conversation reports that pension funds alone own more than two-thirds of the equity of America's 1,000 largest companies, and this does not include mutual funds, trust funds, and so forth. Samuel M. Loescher of Indiana University, in an address to the American Economics Association meeting, December 28, 1987, seemed to reconcile our analysis with Drucker's, pointing out that "pension funds are estimated to own 50% of the common stock of *S&P* 500 corporations." He went on to point out that if one includes institutional investors that commingle in their portfolios tax-deferred 401K and IRA contributions of individuals, then pension funds own 65% of the common stock of these companies.

Blaming everything on the directors would be both unfair and untrue. That so many directors of major corporations gave us their time, candor, and insights indicates their own concerns about their role.

Phrases such as "Made in America" and "The American Way" rang a little less boldly in the 1980s. In business and economic terms, we are no longer the undisputed envy of the world's other industrial nations, nor are we the unquestioned role model to which under- and undeveloped nations aspire. The decline was real and, at least in part, measurable—less certain are the causes and, more important, the cures. We believe this study may illuminate some of the ways in which directors are factors for both good and ill, and how some of the impediments to more effective governance might be removed.

Previous Studies

We began our research mindful of earlier studies of corporate governance.[9] In 1971, for example, Mace described board membership as more of an accolade than an obligation, calling directors "ornaments on a corporate Christmas tree."[10] Directors were usually chosen from the corporation's executives, both retired and active, from more indirectly related sources such as lawyers and bankers, and from successful friends and acquaintances of the CEO—a sort of "old boys' club," with the protection of shareholder interests and evaluation of top management secondary to the role of advising the CEO.

Corporate boards today are very different from the old elitist corps of overseers with limited responsibility. Not only the challenges of the 1980s, but also events of the 1970s, when directors' conduct was scrutinized in cases where corporations engaged in foreign corrupt practices and made questionable political contributions, have forced changes in the

9. See, for example, Charles A. Anderson and Robert W. Anthony, *The New Corporate Directors* (New York: John Wiley, 1986); Stanley C. Vance, *Corporate Leadership, Boards, Directors, and Strategy* (New York: McGraw-Hill, 1983); and James C. Worthy and Robert D. Neushel, *Emerging Issues in Corporate Governance* (Evanston, Ill.: Northwestern University Press, 1983).

10. Myles Mace, *Directors: Myth and Reality* (Boston: Division of Research, Harvard Business School, 1971).

composition and the functioning of boards. Such unsavory activities as bribing foreign officials to keep out competition and paying employees phony "bonuses" that were, after taxes, illegally donated to political candidates[11] prompted critical reports from the American Law Institute and the Business Roundtable, adding weight to the forces for change.[12]

A majority of directors now come from outside the corporation, the number of board committees to facilitate the directors' work has risen, and directors today view their role and their responsibilities with a seriousness and an involvement that were often lacking fifteen or more years ago. The following three directors speak for almost everyone we interviewed:

> In the early years, being invited to join a board was a sign of respect . . . some people served on a lot of boards because the duties were minimal. We weren't given much information before a meeting and even attendance wasn't essential. If you went, it was to listen to management describe its plans. But now that the courts hold directors liable if they don't uphold the business judgment rule, directors have begun to ask for information so they can make informed decisions. They have to be more responsible now—they can't go on 18 boards now, because it's too dangerous.

> Directors today don't want colleagues like the old ones who rubber-stamped management's decisions. You don't want to share responsibilities—or liabilities— with people who don't pull their own weight or do their homework.

> Directors are more forward nowadays. There's no more of the good-old-boy club meeting atmosphere, because of the directors' responsibility and liability. They don't assume something is correct simply because the CEO said it. They want proof he's right. I'm on seven

11. Business Roundtable, *The Role and Composition of the Board of Directors of Large Publicly Owned Corporations* (New York, 1978); and the American Law Institute, *Principles of Corporate Governance: Analysis and Recommendation, Tentative Drafts* (Philadelphia, 1983).

12. George C. Greanias and Duane Windsor, eds., *The Foreign Corrupt Practices Act: Anatomy of a Statute* (Lexington, Mass.: Lexington Books, 1982).

boards, and the directors question deeply at every meeting I attend.

While the functioning of boards has unquestionably improved, our study indicates that further innovations are needed if directors are to be effective governors. Earlier studies were predicated on an historical legal view of the directors' roles and the boards' functioning—a unidimensional, even simplistic, perspective crediting directors with complete understanding of their legal accountability and duties, freedom from other pressures impinging on their responsibilities, and presuming their legal authority powerful enough to permit them to govern. Modern directors, however, reveal a different reality—one in which the ability to carry out their legally defined responsibilities is often impeded: one shaped not only by the job's legal specifications, but by the directors' psychological reasons for serving, by limits on their time, by their understanding of their accountabilities, and by relationships among themselves and with the CEO-chairman. While the real directors' world differs from outside perceptions of it, both are imbedded in the historical legal perspective. Thus, understanding that perspective is important.

The Historical Legal Perspective

The concept of the corporation as a legal entity came to the United States with the merchant adventurers' associations that brought commerce to the American colonies from England.[13] The Elizabethan view of the corporation as an artificial entity created by legal fiat was echoed in U.S. law by Chief Justice Marshall in 1819 in the Dartmouth College case, when he stated, "The corporation is an artificial being, invisible, intangible, and existing only in the contemplation of the law."[14] Under the Constitution the right to incorporate was vested in the states as one of their sovereign powers, a right so strictly adhered to that the railroads, for example, found it necessary to incorporate in each state where they operated.

13. Vance, *Corporate Leadership,* p. 2.
14. *Dartmouth College* v. *Woodward,* 1819.

The idea for a board of directors also had its roots in colonial enterprises, which were governed by a council of peers. Benjamin Franklin and Alexander Hamilton built on the idea to create boards of directors for their eighteenth-century enterprises. As Vance points out, two centuries after Alexander Hamilton established "the first real American corporation," the statement of purpose he gave for directors sounds remarkably modern: "the affairs of the company are to be under the management of 13 directors."[15] The phraseology is similar to that of the General Corporation Law of the State of Delaware, where about 50% of publicly owned corporations are incorporated: "The business and affairs of every corporation organized under this chapter shall be managed by or under the direction of a board of directors. . . ."[16]

As commerce expanded in the late eighteenth and early nineteenth centuries, various states vied to have companies domiciled in their jurisdictions, courting them through the creation of the most liberal laws applying to directors. In this context, "liberal" meant that directors would not be held to the same tight standards as trustees, the so-called prudent man rule. Instead, directors were expected to exercise the *duty of loyalty* and *the duty of care,* and their conduct was judged according to *the business judgment doctrine.* In spite of the evolution of corporate law and legal variations among the states, these principles still remain at the heart of directors' responsibilities in all jurisdictions.[17] For this reason we want to explain them briefly, even though readers with a legal background will recognize that they are the bare bones of a director's legal position and that the business-judgment rule is still evolving, particularly in Delaware. Our advice to our director readers, as in all legal matters, is: When in doubt, consult your corporate counsel.

The duty of loyalty is best exemplified when a director who serves on the boards of two companies finds he or she has a

15. Vance, *Corporate Leadership,* p. 5.
16. *Delaware General Corporation Law Annotated Franchise Tax Law Uniform Limited Partnership Act.* As of February 2, 1988 (Englewood Cliffs, N.J.: Prentice-Hall Legal and Financial Service, 1988).
17. Further, these principles are at the core of the American Bar Association's "Model Business Corporation Act."

conflict between the interests of the two. In such an instance, the court would apply a fairness test in which the director must establish his actions as being appropriately diligent, which is the duty of care. Duty of care, therefore, means using due diligence. Practically, this means the director has an obligation to find out everything that he can that bears on the decision in question. When no conflict is involved, the courts will not interfere with the decisions of the board as long as due care has been exercised, under the business judgment doctrine.[18] However, the business judgment doctrine does not apply when there is a conflict of interest. Nor does it apply when the duty of care has not been exercised, or when there is a breach of the duty of loyalty. In such instances, the courts base their judgment on whether the directors have been intrinsically fair.

In gathering the information needed to exercise business judgment, directors are entitled to rely on their own officers as well as experts. This is one reason why prior studies have placed emphasis on the creation and utilization of committees, and on the availability of information to directors. The board is also protected in delegating to others, although there are specific decisions that cannot be delegated: for example, matters related to dividends, the right to sell the corporation, and mergers and acquisitions.

The capacity to delegate and the fact that the "corporation shall be managed by or *under the direction*" of the board means that one potentially controversial point between managers and directors is the question of the board's activities and decisions compared to those of management. This matter has become particularly important as there have been calls for more active directors. Both the Business Roundtable and the American Law Institute (ALI) have addressed the potential problem by recommending what the duties of directors should be. The Business Roundtable specifies that directors have the following duties:

---

18. While our description focuses on the laws of Delaware, because of its importance as a state of incorporation, the laws of other states are largely consistent with this point. See the American Bar Association Model Corporation Act.

1. Overseeing of management and board selection and succession.
2. Reviewing the company's financial performance and allocating its funds.
3. Overseeing corporate social responsibility.
4. Ensuring compliance with the law.[19]

The American Law Institute provides a different approach to management oversight, but not an incompatible list:

1. Elect, evaluate and, where appropriate, dismiss the principal senior executives.
2. Oversee the conduct of the corporation's business, with a view to evaluation on an ongoing basis, whether the corporation's resources are being managed in a manner consistent with [enhancing shareholder gain, within the law, within ethical considerations, and while directing a reasonable amount of resources to public welfare and humanitarian purposes].
3. Review and approve corporate plans and actions that the board and principal senior executives consider major and changes in accounting principles that the board or principal senior executives consider material.
4. Perform such other functions as are prescribed by law, or assigned to the board under a standard of the corporation.

The board . . . should also have power to:

1. Make recommendations to shareholders.
2. Initiate and adopt major corporate plans, commitments, and actions, and material changes in accounting principles and practices; instruct any committees, officers, and employees; and review the actions of any committee, officer, or other employee.

---

19. Business Roundtable, *The Role and Composition of the Board of Directors of Large Publicly Held Corporations*, p. 3.

3. Act as to all other corporate matters not requiring stockholder approval.[20]

While both groups use the term *oversight*, the meaning differs. The American Law Institute's position is that it's impossible for directors to "manage" the corporation, as the Delaware law stipulates, in the limited time they have. Therefore, directors should carry out oversight of management only through review and evaluations. If management is not performing effectively, the directors should replace it. The Business Roundtable believes directors can be realistically involved in setting broad policy directions by working with the CEO and other top managers, and can play the role envisioned in the Delaware statute. This argument is further clouded by the fact that not all lawyers agree with the American Law Institute's position. Moreover, the difference of opinion has had little impact on how managers and directors actually view their role.

However, two underlying assumptions stand out in the Business Roundtable and the ALI statements. First is the premise that the legal authority provided in Delaware, or for that matter in other states, is adequate for directors to carry out these duties. The Business Roundtable was quite specific on this point: "Political models are not relevant to an organization whose principal function is the provision of goods and services; which must perform this function subject to the discipline of the marketplace and competition, and which is already subject to a host of external constraints, legal, social and political."[21] It is easy to understand why an association of CEOs, the most powerful voices in their companies, would take this position and argue for an organization "which is cohesive, not divided, and which is fast moving, responsive, and flexible rather than bound by excessive bureaucratic regulations or formalities, either internal or external."[22]

Such statements are seductive and seem appropriate to

---

20. American Law Institute, *Principles of Corporate Governance: Analysis and Recommendation*, Draft 2 (Philadelphia, April 13, 1984), pp. 66–67.
21. Business Roundtable, *The Role and Composition of the Board of Directors*, p. 25.
22. Ibid.

the dynamic business climate of the 70s and 80s. They also reflect the preference of these corporate leaders for an organization with no added constraints on their ability to lead. Their jobs are highly complicated and, as the Roundtable argument suggests, their decisions are already constrained by a web of market and other forces.[23] While one can empathize, it is clear the Roundtable is implicitly arguing that directors have no barriers to exercising their legal authority. In recent personal conversations with representatives of the Business Roundtable who are concerned with corporate governance, we found them explicit on this point. The directors, most of whom are also CEOs of companies, feel there are major impediments to carrying out their duties.

The second underlying assumption stands out most clearly in the ALI list of duties—directors are accountable to the shareholders. Their duty is to protect shareholders' interests and provide an adequate return on their investment. Such an assumption is consistent with Delaware court decisions that have ruled that directors are fiduciaries in relation to the corporation and its shareholders, not as individuals, but as a class.[24] In this regard, too, Delaware has been historically consistent with the laws of the other states.

From this perspective, the directors' duties are clear, at least in legal theory. Perhaps in more halcyon times, when the shareholders were individuals, such as the proverbial "little old lady from Peoria," it was also clear in reality. But in an era of institutional ownership, leveraged buyouts, and unfriendly takeovers, understanding who the shareholders are and where their real interests lie is even more difficult. Further, corporations are a fundamental institution in our society and economy. They have many other stakeholders: customers, employees, governments, lenders, suppliers, and communities. According to Delaware law, if directors look out for the long-term interests of shareholders they will also be deemed to have taken care of the corporations' other stakeholders. However, in recent years, in response to unfriendly takeovers,

---

23. The impact of such constraints was demonstrated in Gordon Donaldson and Jay W. Lorsch, *Decision Making at the Top* (New York: Basic Books, 1983).
24. *Delaware General Corporation Law*, p. 141.3.

seventeen states, not including Delaware, have enacted laws empowering directors to consider stakeholders other than the shareholders.[25]

The key tenets of the traditional legal perspective, then, are that directors are legally responsible for the management of the corporation; that they are expected to exercise the duties of loyalty, care, and good business judgment. Their primary accountability is to shareholders, although there has been change in this regard in states other than Delaware. These principles are the foundation upon which the structure of corporate governance is built. However, the data gathered from directors indicate that this structure has some significant shortcomings. This conclusion is due less to inherent flaws in the traditional legal foundation than to the fact that this perspective doesn't recognize many of the human and managerial realities directors encounter as they try to govern.[26]

The Director's Reality

From the directors' perspective, their legal authority to manage the corporation is a clear mandate, but problems arise as they try to act upon that authority. To understand their difficulty, we need a closer look at the concept of governance. In a corporation, as in the public arena, governing involves the exercise of authority or power toward a particular end. Thus,

25. James A. Hanks, "Recent Legislation on D&O Liability Limitation," *The Business Lawyer* (August 1988) lists: Arizona, Idaho, Illinois, Indiana, Kentucky, Maine, Minnesota, Missouri, Nebraska, New Mexico, New York, Ohio, Pennsylvania, and Wisconsin. James P. Melican, senior vice president and general counsel for International Paper Company, added in private correspondence, January 1989, Connecticut, Louisiana, and Tennessee.

26. The data about the directors' reality was gathered in several ways. First, 100 outside directors of *Standard & Poor's* 400 companies were randomly selected to be interviewed. Of those, about 80 agreed to be, and were, interviewed. Additionally several legal experts were also interviewed for their viewpoint; similarly, a number of British CEOs were interviewed to get their perspectives on U.S. boards as compared to their own. Questionnaires were sent to 3,000 of the directors of these companies, and the response rate was 31%. The S&P's 400 companies were selected because we wanted to focus on manufacturing companies because of the difficulties these companies have had in the 70s and 80s. However, the *Standard & Poor's* list also included some service companies. Finally, about 35 other directors and CEOs were interviewed in the development of the four cases described in Chapters 6 and 7.

to govern effectively, directors must have enough power to influence the course of corporate direction, a power that is, at the least, slightly greater than the power of those the directors are to govern—the company's top managers and the employees who report to them.

As obvious as this may seem, we say it with some trepidation, recognizing that for many readers, "power" is an emotionally charged term, conjuring up images of struggles and fights for control. We use the term not in that sense, but to convey the very essence of a process of governance—to be able to govern one must have the power to make decisions and to enforce their execution. The exercise of power may be subtle and unobtrusive, as it is in most corporations, but it must be exercised if there is to be true governance.

Previous discussions of corporate governance have avoided references to the concept of power, preferring to stress the need for outside directors to be *independent*. However, independence means freedom from unresolvable conflicts of interests with other companies (the duty of loyalty), and autonomy vis-à-vis management. In our view, being a truly independent director means having sufficient power to govern.

In the corporate boardroom, there are multiple sources of power, of which the directors' legal authority is just one. Others are the confidence to express one's ideas and views, knowledge and information about the matter under discussion, and control over the agenda and the discussion process. There is power in unity, too, whenever a majority of the board stands firmly behind a particular position. But essentially, directors are at a disadvantage when these sources of boardroom power are realistically considered. The CEO-chairman usually has greater knowledge and information and controls both the meeting agenda and the discussion process. Often, he has been instrumental in selecting the other directors. In truth, other than their legal mandate, the directors' only power advantage is their capacity to act as a group by reaching a consensus, but doing this requires group cohesion and time for discussion, often scarce commodities in the typical boardroom.

The directors, in essence, gain the power to govern through the consent of the governed, which may sound like a laudable democratic objective but which is inconsistent with the intent of corporate law. Fortunately, on most boards, in normal times, the CEO-chairman tries not to sabotage his or her board's effectiveness. In time of crisis, however, the implicit understanding between the CEO-chairman and the directors can collapse like a house of cards, particularly when the views of the two sides are in conflict.

We begin our examination of this governance reality in Chapter 2 with a description of the men and women who serve as directors, how they are selected, and why they serve on boards.

In Chapter 3, we examine another power constraint directors face, a confusion among them about the exact definition of their accountability and the reasons for that confusion. Given the importance of public corporations in American society, we also examine the desirability of holding to a traditional legal perspective that expects directors to devote a majority of attention to shareholders.

While there is concern, from the legal perspective, with the division of responsibility between directors and managers, we find in Chapter 4 that, in actuality, the two parties have worked out a mutually satisfactory modus operandi. The problem is that directors can have difficulty mustering sufficient power to carry out their self-defined responsibilities, which include the most important tasks of selecting, evaluating, rewarding, and, if necessary, removing the CEO.

Obviously, there are two aspects to the power imbalance, one being the lack of director power, while on the opposite side are the factors that give the chairman-CEO so much influence. In Chapter 5 we identify a CEO's power sources relative to that of the directors in the normal conduct of the corporation affairs, then recapitulate the directors' power constraints and assess the balance of power between directors and CEOs in normal times.

The normal power relationship between the chairman-CEO and the directors is the springboard from which directors must act in times of crisis. In Chapters 6 and 7 we use crises facing boards at four corporations to explore how board members deal with both internally and externally caused crises, and those that occur suddenly and dramatically, as well as those that emerge more gradually. While there are variations in how difficult the directors' problems are in each situation, there is a common theme. When boards had to act without CEO support, or in opposition to the CEO, lack of power inhibited them, delaying their ability to act. Further, a successful resolution depended upon the serendipitous emergence of a leader from among the outside directors. The obvious question is, What happens on boards where the directors are not so lucky? In our view, the present governance system leaves too much to chance, and allows crises to drag on longer than is good for any of the stakeholders. As we have seen, too many corporations simultaneously having crises causes problems for the whole economy.

The Need for Change

This concern, along with a recognition that more effective governance means more relative power for directors, leads us in Chapter 8 to recommend several basic changes in the current system of corporate governance. These innovations will require changes in state laws and in the bylaws of corporations, as well as in the rules governing stock exchanges.

Being pragmatic, we recognize that such changes will be difficult to achieve and slow in coming. We also understand that many CEOs and many directors, whether CEOs or not, may feel the changes are too extreme. For those reasons, we also propose a more modest set of recommendations—"changes within the system"—that we believe would do much to place directors in a better position to govern, and that could be implemented by the CEOs and directors of any company, within their present legal authority.

Chapter 2

The Directors

Our first step in explaining the reality of corporate governance will be to examine who serves on boards, how they are selected, and what motivates them to take board seats. This analysis will enable us to evaluate statements such as the following, made by an active CEO, also serving as a director of other companies:

> There has been a growing predominance of outside directors who are there not only to provide a new perspective to top management's thinking, but also to provide the necessary oversight only possible from an outsider.

This comment reflects a general consensus that an increasing proportion of outside directors is a positive step. While not disputing the trend, our data reveal that despite serious motives for joining boards, many directors still feel they are serving at the pleasure of the CEO-chairman. This is true even though 74% of directors are now outsiders, of whom 69% are nonmanagement personnel with no other contact with the company. The remaining 5% are indirectly affiliated with the company as bankers, lawyers, or retired executives.[1] Exact comparative data are scarce, but considering that in

1. Heidrick & Struggles, Inc., *The Changing Board* (Boston, 1987), p. 3.

1938 only 50% of U.S. companies had a majority of outside directors, and by 1979 that proportion had grown to 83%,[2] we can assume a sharp increase in the number of outside directors per individual company.

Demographics of Outside Directors

As the percentage of outside directors has increased, the challenge of locating qualified candidates has grown. For the most part, directors form a relatively uniform pool. Of all *Fortune 1000* directors, 93.8% are white males[3] and two-thirds are over 55 years old;[4] 63% of all board members are CEOs of other corporations.[5] One director's explanation typifies the thinking of many:

> *I think CEOs like to have other CEOs on their boards because they feel they have had similar experiences and they are meeting the same challenges. Furthermore, other CEOs tend to have a better idea of the sometimes imprecise limits between overseeing the functions of the company and the management of that enterprise. It is easy for board members to slip across that line, and CEOs do it less than others because they don't want their directors doing it on their boards.*

Such comments reveal both the pros and cons for asking so many CEOs to join boards. On the positive side, other CEOs *do* understand the difficulties of leading a complex company and are excellent resources on a board. Not only are they knowledgeable in making decisions and judgments, they can be useful advisers to the CEO-chairman. The danger, however, is that CEOs may play by the Golden Rule—doing unto other CEOs as they would have done unto them—resulting in the "imprecise

---

2. Murray L. Weidenbaum, *Strengthening the Corporate Board: A Constructive Response to Harsh Takeovers* (St. Louis, Mo.: Center for the Study of American Business, Washington University, 1985), p. 20.
3. Heidrick & Struggles, *The Changing Board.*
4. Directorship Databank at Directorship Publications, Inc.
5. Our own survey.

limit" between the board's role and management's, tending too often to be drawn in management's favor.

In addition, though CEOs are the most desired board members, the pool of candidates is finite. Given his or her other responsibilities, there is a limit to the number of boards a CEO can join. Not surprisingly, CEOs decline three times as many board invitations as do directors from other professions. Sixty-two percent of all CEOs have declined at least one invitation to join a corporate board, compared with only 22% among all outside directors.[6]

Evidence indicates there aren't enough CEOs to go around, as some rudimentary mathematics explains (see Table 2-1):

Table 2-1[a]

Average number of directors per board	=	13[b]
Outside directors (69%) per board	=	9
Outside directors needed for 1,000 companies	=	9,000
63% of whom are expected to be CEOs	=	5,670[c]

a. Since the surveys cited are for *Fortune* 1000 companies, calculations are based on those companies.
b. Heidrick & Struggles, *The Changing Board*, p. 2.
c. Our own survey.

The active CEOs of *Fortune* 1000 companies would each have to serve on almost six boards to meet the demand. In the past, active CEOs may have joined six or more boards, but the increasing complexity of both a CEO's and a director's job has made such a heavy commitment impossible and unwise. Even if the pool were expanded to include more retired CEOs and CEOs of nonmanufacturing companies, there would still be a shortage, a fact suggesting that those concerned about the selection of new outside directors will have to look beyond CEOs for their candidates. While this may complicate the task of locating qualified directors, it should also reduce the dangers of overreliance on CEOs.

6. According to *Korn Ferry's International Board of Directors Survey*, 1987, 22.2% of prospective directors declined an invitation to serve. According to Heidrick & Struggles, *The Changing Board*, 1987, 5 of 8 (62%) chairmen-CEOs indicated they declined an invitation to serve.

Selecting and Electing Directors

The discussion above naturally raises the issue of how outside directors are selected for membership on a particular board. Legally, it is a multistep process, beginning when the incumbent directors search for potential nominees and ending when the shareholders elect those who are nominated by the directors or by the shareholders themselves. Traditionally, however, in most companies, selecting directors has been the exclusive responsibility of the CEO, who chose the candidates, then recommended them to the board for its approval. The sense of the CEO's ownership of the selection process was exemplified by how often one heard a CEO referring to "my board." Even today, many CEOs are a major influence in the selection of directors, and many still refer to the board as "my directors," but the trend is moving away from such CEO dominance, mainly because of the emergence of nominating committees. In our survey, 84% of the directors reported that the boards on which they served have such committees. Nevertheless, in many companies, these committees still have limited influence compared to that of the CEO.

We can best understand the situation if we divide the selection and election process into its component parts: identifying candidates, evaluating them, nominating them, electing them. Beginning with the first step, 55% of the directors reported that the CEO was the major source of ideas for new candidates, while only one-third considered the nominating committee the most important source. Furthermore, when the CEO suggested a candidate, 11% of the directors indicated that that person was always accepted, while 57% said the CEO's choice was accepted "most of the time." Similarly, 42% of the directors reported that the CEO's candidates were rarely rejected by the nominating committee.

Directors do feel that they have more influence on the evaluation process once a potential candidate has been identified. On a five-point scale (1 = a great deal of influence to 5 = little influence), directors rated their influence in candidate evaluation at 2.02 while they rated their influence in the formal nomination of new members at 2.45. A director spoke for many when he described the changing process:

> The CEO used to make most of the suggestions for new directors and tried to create a board "in his own image," but now this responsibility is shifting to the nominating committee because board members are demanding that they have more impact on all aspects of corporate governance.

A second director attributed the trend to the problems of the 1970s:

> I think that the evolution has been away from the CEO controlling the [selection] process; it is now a much more structured system. I think the idea was that in order to elicit the broader confidence of the investing public, and to maintain an image of objectivity, the CEO couldn't appear to be selecting his own pals to join the board and thus insulate himself from the kinds of judgment and questioning that might otherwise be present. I think this has been an evolutionary change, but I would say that the rate of change accelerated in the early to mid-70s because of a few corporate failures and other crises.

The changes in the selection process can be traced not only to public pressures and concern for the corporate image, but also to how directors view their responsibilities. Directors today seek greater involvement because whoever is selected will impact on the board's effectiveness. One board member commented:

> I think companies are changing or, more important, companies have changed. There is a new awareness on the part of major corporations that started way back with the foreign corrupt practices activity and the campaign fund concerns. Boards now realize that they really have to be a much more open window in terms of their responsibilities to the public, to shareholders, to employees and so forth—for their own sake's as much as the company's.

In spite of these changes, the directors' influence is still limited in comparison to the CEO's. For the most part, there is a division in responsibility between the CEO, who identifies new candidates, and the nominating committee or full board, which evaluates and formally nominates candidates. Two directors spoke for others in explaining the CEO's predominance. The first, a retired CEO:

> I think the strongest person in the process is definitely the CEO. He is the executive officer of the company, and directors are not really equipped to perform those functions. There is a certain amount of mechanics to the investigation because there's no point selecting someone with a legal conflict of interest.

The second, a lawyer:

> The CEO has a very strong hand in the whole process and usually has strong preferences as far as candidates are concerned, at least to the extent of giving the nominating committee two or three names he'd like them to look at. I think most CEOs feel, justifiably, that they are entitled to select people of judgment, but who will feel also sympathetic to them.

Thus, though outside directors are now more involved, the power still rests in the hands of the CEO. References to "my directors" may be diminishing, but they have not yet disappeared.

The shareholders are obviously not involved until the election phase, and even at this point, their impact is negligible. Most elections offer only one slate of directors. For example, in 99.9% of corporate elections held in 1985, only one slate was offered.[7] Two slates might be offered, but only when a party seeking to gain control of the company submits an alternate slate.[8] While the single-slate election resembles a pre-glasnost Russian election and seems inconsistent with our democratic values, there doesn't seem to be a practical alternative. First, since it's often difficult to find enough candidates to fill one slate, it would be next to impossible to find enough for

7. Edward J. Epstein, *Who Owns the Corporation? Management vs. Shareholders* (New York: Twentieth Century Fund, 1986), p. 13.

8. There have been a few examples of institutions using their power of ownership to influence board composition in takeover battles, but these hardly seem to represent a trend, as recently discussed by Stratford P. Sherman in *Fortune* magazine, "Pushing Corporate Boards to be Better" (July 18, 1988), p. 58.

two. Obviously, the potential embarrassment of losing a contested election would discourage many competent individuals from standing. Further, few shareholders would have any way to identify and contact potential write-in candidates, if they wanted to offer an alternate slate. The increasing turnover of stock ownership also suggests that many shareholders have no long-term interest in the corporation. Generally, such investors are unconcerned about who serves on the board and, when dissatisfied with corporate performance, will sell their shares rather than try to influence board representation.

The composition of most boards is, therefore, still heavily influenced by the CEO, with growing influence from other directors, particularly those on the nominating committee. Although one can be critical of the CEO's influence, there seems little question that the present system is finding highly qualified, distinguished individuals to serve on boards. For example, the Appendix to this chapter lists the directors, randomly selected, who agreed to be interviewed. A quick perusal of their names and titles suggests the high caliber of those serving on American boards. With the exception of our concern about the overreliance on CEOs, the right people seem to be ending up on boards, and their purpose in serving is serious. This will become clearer as we examine why such busy and highly qualified individuals find joining boards so rewarding.

Joining and Serving

The most pressing issue a director faces in deciding to join a board is whether he or she has the time to serve (see Table 2-2). Senior-level executives, lawyers, government officials, and academics shoulder a wide array of responsibilities that limit their time for board membership, especially since the average director devotes 14 days a year, including preparation, travel, and committee meetings, to each board on which he or she serves.[9]

---

9. Heidrick & Struggles, The Changing Board, p. 9.

Table 2-2
Reasons for Refusing Board Membership

(Scale: 1 = Very Influential	5 = Not Influential)
Lack of time	1.72
Meeting conflicts	2.19
Conflict of interest	2.30
Could not play useful role	2.68
No interest in firm's industry	2.78
Uncertainty about firm's future	2.97
Personal liability	2.97

However, different individuals assess both the time needed for, and the responsibilities of, board membership differently. At one extreme is the retired CEO of one of the world's largest corporations:

> I'm on ten boards at the moment. It's not a big deal; it's like ten half-days a month. I wasn't on ten boards when I was CEO, though. I'm a great believer that you cannot be on a lot of boards and run a company at the same time. Once I stepped down as CEO, at 60, and decided I didn't want to go to Washington, I decided that being a director was a good idea.

Each board, he says, requires only six days a year, less than half the average time his peers report.

Another retired CEO serves on only two boards besides his own, because he weighed board responsibilities more heavily:

> There are two reasons why I said "yes" to these two boards and have said "no" to all the rest. One, you have so little time that you really can't take on more than two if you want to do the job properly. Two, these two are convenient to my office and my schedule.

An active and distinguished Washington lawyer agreed:

> It's a considerable distraction for a lawyer, I think. It certainly takes close to 20 days a year in terms of travel, telephone conferences, meetings, and preparation, to be an effective director. This is definitely a deterrent. A famous judge once said that no active person

*could possibly serve on more than two boards at any
one time and still make a positive contribution. The
most I have ever sat on is four, and that's a hell of a
heavy load to carry at one time.*

Given the variations in personal experiences and outside activities, as well as varying perceptions about their responsibilities, it isn't surprising that board members have different
opinions as to how many boards they can and should join. The
limits of time are real for even the most capable and energetic
individuals, and often constrain a director's ability to govern.

Even if a candidate has time, he or she often faces such
problems as conflicting meeting dates or a conflict of interest
(see Table 2-2). No individual can be in two places at once, nor
can he or she serve if there is a conflict of interest, such as an
overlap in product line, or a strong buyer-seller relationship.

A retired CEO described his thoughts this way:

*When I evaluate an offer to join a board, first I de-
termine whether . . . there is a conflict of interest. Next I
have to find out whether there will be a conflict of days.
I've been asked to join a couple of boards, and even before we determine whether or not a mutual interest exists, we've found that I couldn't because they met on
the same day [as my board]. In other cases, due to the
breadth of our company's product line, I've been unable
to serve because of conflict of interest.*

Many potential candidates confront at least one of these concerns—lack of time, overlapping meeting dates, or conflict of
interest—compounding the problem of finding eligible directors, especially those active CEOs for whom time pressures are
likely to be greatest.

Other, less prevalent, reasons why qualified candidates
refuse board membership are more personal (see Table 2-2)
and linked to whether individuals feel they can play a useful
role or whether they are interested in the corporation's activities. Tied for last place on the list is concern about legal liability, which is particularly surprising in light of the recent
speculations that qualified outside directors are declining invitations to join boards because of concern about personal

liability.[10] Based on our data, directors are less worried about liability than they are about time. Our conclusion is supported by a 1986 study in which only 14% of the directors surveyed who turned down a board seat did so because of increasing liability levels, whereas 65% did so because of "the time commitment."[11] Apparently, directors don't let legal risks stop them, any more than a jockey allows the risk of injury to keep him out of a race. Such risks go with the territory.

Two directors reflected this prevalent view of legal liability:

I have never not been entangled in a lawsuit; I have had at least one pending against me as a director since I first began serving. It's absurd. I have never had a judgment against me, but you know you have to keep looking over your shoulder and wondering what's going to sneak up next.

The pressures concerning fiduciary responsibility leave directors living in a fishbowl. You have to stand in line to sue them, but you just can't worry about that.

Having learned why potential candidates turn down board invitations, it's also important to understand why they accept. Although it may seem surprising, directors join a board because, above all else, they seek intellectual stimulation and new ideas (see Table 2-3).

Table 2-3
Reasons for Joining a Board

(Scale: 1 = Most Important 5 = Least Important)	
Quality of top management	1.78
Opportunity to learn	1.93
Challenge as director	2.08
Prestige of the firm	2.22
Potential growth of the firm	2.41
Opportunity to work with board members	2.66
Personal prestige	2.98
Compensation	3.61
Major stock ownership	4.37

10. For example see Heidrick & Struggles, *The Changing Board,* p. 1.
11. *Korn Ferry's Board of Directors Annual Survey,* 1987, p. 11.

The quality of top management is the most important variable in their decision because it has an impact on nearly every other reason for joining a board and, specifically, upon the second most important one, the opportunity to learn. If the CEO and other top managers are ineffective, it is unlikely that there will be many opportunities to learn or be challenged, that the firm will enjoy either a noteworthy reputation or much promise for growth, or that the other directors will be stimulating. One director put it all together:

> Serving on a board is a way to see how somebody else is doing the same thing you're doing. I usually look at the company to see if they are a strong, growing firm, but I also look at the senior people to see if they're interesting and if they'll be involved in interesting problems.

Serving as outside directors of other companies allows active CEOs to learn from their peers, as well as from exposure to a wider array of business problems. Two CEOs made this point:

> The problems one encounters serving as an outside director may be very valuable for a CEO in running his own firm. The situation will never be exactly the same, but the insights one can gain will definitely be of some value when looking at a merger or an LBO.

> I've learned a terrific amount, and basically I think directors ought to pay to serve on boards because you learn so much about situations that you, in turn, become faced with. I can give you a long list of situations I've handled better here at my company because I've been through them or seen them or thought them through elsewhere as an outside board member. It's a great opportunity.

Almost all the directors who were CEOs felt the same, enjoying the opportunity to learn about other business situations and to compare them with experiences in their own companies. CEOs, however, were not the only ones to stress the importance of the learning opportunity. An educator commented: "Well, I guess I thought I could learn something. I had spent all of my life with eleemosynary institutions of one sort or another and I thought I might be able to learn a little bit about the discipline of having to worry about the bottom line." The president of a major nonprofit institution concurred:

> *You really learn something through all of it. You learn an incredible amount about parts of the industrial life of this country, and this is inextricably linked to the world economy. To the extent that you prize both freedom and economic opportunity, which are really the engines that have proven to be the most effective over time, why not know more about them and contribute in any way possible?*

When asked to rate the personal benefits derived from serving on corporate boards, the directors' responses were highly consistent with these comments and their reasons for joining (see Table 2-4). Learning was the paramount benefit, and some of it came from being exposed to new business situations.

Apart from intellectual stimulation, some directors valued other benefits. One educator, for example, commented on the expansion of his window on the world:

> *There are several reasons [why I serve]. First of all, I enjoy it; actually I find it fascinating. It's a break from what I normally do, especially from the university's standpoint. I get to see a part of the world that I wouldn't have the opportunity to see otherwise, and I get to know people whom I would not otherwise know. I think that all of the universities with which I have*

Table 2-4
Personal Benefits Derived from Board Membership

(Scale: 1 = Most Important 5 = Least Important)	
Opportunity to learn	1.57
Seeing new businesses	1.86
Establishing contacts to enhance other business relationships	2.90
Opportunity to contribute to society	3.00
Compensation	3.46

ever been associated have benefited in some way from the contacts I have made as a corporate director.

A retired CEO spoke about the satisfaction, in both a narrow and a broad sense, of serving:

> *I enjoy having the opportunity to make an intellectual contribution. I like to see institutions grow and I feel that I'm doing something worthwhile for society. That all sounds sort of hollow when you say it, but the truth of the matter is that we all have a bit of pro bono in our blood and, for the most part, the experience is pleasant.*

Another director, a CEO, felt an obligation to help make the governance system work:

> *If we want the system to work, I have to be willing to serve on other people's boards. If I were to say no all the time to all of the requests that I receive, then obviously the result would be the attitude: if he doesn't want to play ball with me, then I won't play with him. I think it is important that the leaders of major corporations are aware of how this delicate balance operates.*

Such broader concerns are natural for men and women in their fifties and sixties, a stage of their lives where they want to contribute more generally to the world at large and, more specifically, to the condition of the institutions they will pass on to the next generation. Serving as a director is one avenue for fulfilling this goal.

It may seem surprising that the least important consideration in deciding whether or not to join a board, and in the benefits of serving, were the financial rewards (see Tables 2-3 and 2-4). However, with a little reflection, the reasons are apparent. Most active individuals who join boards earn salaries many times larger than directors' fees and, because most directors are in their fifties and sixties, they've earned high salaries for many years.[12] One director, who was also an active consul-

---

12. The average annual cash compensation of outside directors of the *Fortune* 1000 companies was $22,000 in 1987. The most highly paid outside directors, who were on boards of those companies with sales of more than $2 billion, received an average of $32,600 annually. Heidrick & Struggles, *The Changing Board,* p. 8.

tant, remarked:

> *I look at the risk/reward trade-off and the reward in all of this is psychological . . . not compensation. Directors are totally underpaid for what they contribute. The fee is peanuts when you consider that one good idea is equal to 10 years of directors' fees.*

Of all the reasons directors cited for joining boards, the one rated lowest was major stock ownership (see Table 2-3). Not one director spoke about his own investments as a reason for joining or a benefit from serving on boards. While most board members do own shares of the company's stock, many own only a token number. Their attitude may disturb those who believe in the importance of financial and economic incentives. Certainly, if one examines the traditional legal perspective, the only references to rewards for directors are their fees and ownership of stock. However, the reality is different. Their rewards are intrinsic and psychological, and such rewards are more powerful than economic ones. The implications of directors' lack of concern with stock ownership, in terms of their views on accountability, will be discussed in future chapters.

Conclusions

America's boards are made up of, by and large, responsible and dedicated directors who take their duties seriously. They serve primarily for intellectual stimulation, increased knowledge, and a desire to leave the corporation stronger for their involvement. We found no dilettantes in our interviews, nor any whose primary purpose was personal financial gain.

The CEO's role in selecting directors, while still a factor in stacking the power deck in his or her favor, is less predominant as more nominating committees allow directors to participate in the process. We see a need, however, for greater director involvement, as well as a need to widen the pool of potential candidates, thus moving away from the current reliance on outside CEOs.

Given the changing nature of shareholders, evolving state laws, and the critical role of America's corporations in both domestic and global terms, perhaps the most important task directors face may be keeping their eyes fixed firmly on the long-term health of the corporation and the economy.

We shall next describe how directors view this issue of accountability.

Appendix

Persons Interviewed about Their Experiences on Boards of Directors*

Sir Robert W. Adam, Executive Vice President
British Petroleum

M. Bernard Aidinoff, Partner
Sullivan & Cromwell, Attorneys at Law

Sir Geoffrey Allen, Executive Vice President
Unilever, N.V.

Warren M. Anderson, former CEO
Union Carbide Corporation

H. Brewster Atwater, Jr., Chairman and CEO
General Mills, Inc.

Michael H. Bader, Partner
Haley, Bader & Potts, Attorneys at Law

H. Furlong Baldwin, Chairman and CEO
Mercantile Bankshares Corporation

James R. Barker, Chief Executive Officer
Moore McCormick Resources Corporation

Joseph W. Barr, Partner
J & J Company

Richard Barrett, Managing Director
Salomon Brothers

W. Cecil Bauer, former Chairman
South Central Bell Telephone Company

Benjamin F. Biaggini, former Chairman
Southern Pacific Corporation

Theodore M. Black, CEO
Walter J. Black, Inc.

Frank Borman, Vice Chairman
Texas Air Corporation

B. A. Bridgewater, Jr., Chairman and CEO
The Brown Group, Inc.

Frank P. Brunetta, CEO
Nygene Corporation

Brian P. Burns, Partner
Burns & Whitehead, Attorneys at Law

Philip Caldwell, Senior Managing Director
Shearson Lehman Brothers, Inc.

Donald C. Carrol, former Dean
The Wharton School of the University of Pennsylvania

Frank T. Cary, Chairman of the Executive Committee
International Business Machines

Andrew J. Chitiea, Senior Vice President
The Signal Companies, Inc.

Clark M. Clifford, Partner
Clifford & Warnke, Attorneys at Law

Paul J. Collins, Executive Vice President
Citicorp

Andrew Crean, President
Andy's Recreational Vehicles

Trammell Crow, Founding Partner
Trammell Crow Company

Lloyd Cutler, Partner
Wilmer, Cutler & Pickering, Attorneys at Law

Raymond V. Cyr, President
Bell Canada Enterprises

J. J. Daniels, formerly of counsel
Pajcic & Pajcic, Attorneys at Law

Charles deBretteville, former Chairman
Bank of California

A. Jean De Grandpre, Chairman and CEO
Bell Canada Enterprises

James F. Dickason, Managing General Partner
Newhall Investments Properties

G. Morris Dorrance, Jr., Chairman and CEO
Corestates Financial Corporation

Robert Ebert, M.D., President—Millbank Memorial Fund
and former Dean—Harvard Medical School

John W. Ellis, Chairman and CEO
Puget Sound Power & Light Company

Nicholas Evans, Senior Vice President
Bristol-Myers Company

James Farley, Senior Chairman
Booz, Allen & Hamilton, Inc.

W. T. Fleming, Partner
Vinson & Elkins, Attorneys at Law

Gerald R. Ford, former President
United States of America

Mario J. Formichella, Partner
Arthur Young & Company

Gaylord Freeman, former Chairman
First National Bank of Chicago

Arthur Furer, former Chairman
Bank Leu

Jarobin Gilbert, Executive Vice President
NBC, Inc.

Henry Goodrich, CEO
SONAT, Inc.

Peter Gordon, former Chairman
Stelco, Inc.

Edmund Haggar, Chairman
Haggar Corporation

Darrell H. Hamric, Director
Centex Corporation

Arthur G. Hansen, Ph.D., former Chancellor
Texas A & M University

Barbara Hauptfurer, Professional
Director

Vernon Heath, CEO
Rosemont, Inc.

Henry B. Henley, Jr., retired Chairman
Cluett, Peabody & Co.

Leo Herzel, Partner
Mayer Brown & Platt, Attorneys at Law

Melvill C. Hill, Executive Vice President
Sears, Roebuck & Co.

Sir Christopher Hoag, Chairman—Reuters
Chief Executive Officer—Courtaulds Ltd.

John J. Horan, former CEO
Merck & Company

Shirley M. Hufstedler, Partner
Hufstedler, Miller, Carlson & Bardsley, Attorneys at Law

Glen Ireland II, Director
Russel Corporation

Howard R. Johnson, Director
Sealed Power Corporation

Edward R. Kane, former Chairman and CEO
E. I. Du Pont de Nemours & Company

James D. Kemper, Chairman and CEO
Commerce Bancshares, Inc.

John J. Kerrigan, President
Transport Workers Union of America

Robert H. Knight, Partner
Shearman & Sterling, Attorneys at Law

Mervyn Lahn, CEO
Canada Trust

Sir Hector Laing, Chairman
United Biscuit, PLC

Donald E. Lasater, Chairman and CEO
Mercantile Bank

Claudine Malone, President
Financial and Management Consulting, Inc.

Alexander Massad, Executive Vice President
Mobil Oil Corporation

Charles P. Moreton, Chairman
Commet Resources, Inc.

Thomas D. Paine, former Director
National Aeronautics and Space Administration

Jane C. Pfeiffer, former Chairman
National Broadcasting Company

Charles Pistor, CEO
Republic National Bank

Arthur Rasmussen, Chairman
Household International, Inc.

William Rushton, Chairman and CEO
Protective Life Insurance

Walter Scott, former Executive Vice President
NBC, Inc.

Franklin A. Thomas, President
The Ford Foundation

Richard M. Thompson, Chairman and CEO
Toronto Dominion Bank

Walter M. Vannoy, CEO
Babcock & Wilcox

Donald G. Willmot, Chairman
The Molson Companies, Ltd.

Otto Wolff von Amerongen, Chairman
Otto Wolff AG

Walter Wriston, former Chairman
Citicorp & Citibank N.A.

*Titles listed are those at the time of interviews, 1986–1987.

Chapter 3

The Directors' Constituents

The directors of a large company are gathered around the boardroom table, discussing management's proposal to adopt a "southern strategy" for the manufacturing facilities of its major division. The proposal involves gradually closing older, unionized plants in three northern urban areas, and building new facilities in the South, which would be nonunion, at least initially, thereby lowering labor costs. As the discussion continues, various directors ask questions or offer opinions about the proposal's merits.

But most striking to an objective observer would be the confusion about what criteria should be used to judge the proposal. Some directors are concerned about the proposal's impact on the present northern work force. Others question whether the nonunionized southern workers could produce a quality product, how long it might take, and what impact there might be on customers. Interspersed are references to "doing what is best for the shareholders," but no clear statement defines how to judge the shareholders' interests. Nor is mention made of the importance of the proposal for the company's long-term position in an increasingly competitive global marketplace.

Such discussions are typical in many boardrooms because directors usually don't share a strong consensus about accountabilities to various constituencies and, therefore, about

their purposes in serving. Further, the norm in most boardrooms is to avoid discussing such matters. The problem is that
the board's power to govern is affected by the extent to which
members have a strong consensus about shared purposes.[1]
The more directors explicitly agree about in whose interests
they are governing, the more they will feel empowered as a
group. Common purposes facilitate both the focus and coordi-
nation of discussions, giving a clear direction that helps ener-
gize individual board members for whom a specific directorship is not a major occupation. Most outside directors have
to shed the preoccupations with their principal occupation
when they enter a boardroom. The clearer they are about their
purposes as directors, the easier the transition. In the boardroom a clearly shared set of goals provides a criterion for members to use in comparing alternatives in discussions and decision making.

The confusion about accountabilities seems surprising in
light of the widely accepted belief that directors are legally
accountable to the shareholders alone. Directors *do* believe the
shareholders are their most important constituents when
reaching decisions (see Table 3-1), but concern for the corporation's long-term future ranked a close second. Other considerations varied among individuals, but in general were less
important. In spite of these generalizations, on the basis of our

Table 3-1
Factors in Directors' Decisions

(The lower the score, the higher the importance)	
Shareholders in general	1.87
Company's long-term future	2.20
CEO's opinion	3.38
Legal requirements	3.43
Customers and suppliers	4.17
Responsibilities to the public	4.25
Competitors in industry	4.61
Employees—not top management	4.90
Management's well-being	5.10
Own investment	7.10

1. Richard Hackman, "The Psychology of Self-Management in Organizations," in
M. S. Pallack and R. O. Perloff, eds., *Psychology and Work: Productivity Change
and Employment* (Washington, D.C.: American Psychological Association,
1986), pp. 102–103.

interviews with directors, we identified three different groups, the first of which we call the traditionalists.

The Traditionalists

These directors adhere to a strict belief in the primacy of the shareholder and decline to recognize that conflicts exist between their traditional legal perspective and that of other constituencies. They are, in our experience, a true minority, and if we question the narrowness of their perspective, we question neither the integrity nor the competence they bring to boardrooms. They have no doubts: in the land of the corporation, the shareholder is king.

Some traditional directors expressed their views thus:

> We all have a stewardship and we represent the shareholders. Our principal responsibility is the election and overseeing of a competent CEO, who is capable of maximizing the shareholders' investment. That hasn't changed over time.

> The conflict between the company's long-term interest and that of the shareholders happens all the time, but a director is legally obligated to act on the shareholder's behalf, so you just have to hope that the two will balance out if you exercise your best judgment.

> It depends upon the issue, but you're always number one, representing the shareholder. It is clear that when you're looking at an issue you're always looking from the shareholder's perspective.

> You don't really have much choice. A director is responsible first and foremost to the shareholders. . . .

If everyone in the boardrooms of America agreed with the traditionalists and understood what the shareholders wanted, the problems we see today wouldn't exist. But most directors hold a more complicated view, believing that in addition to their accountability to the shareholders, of vital importance is the long-term future of the company (see Table 3-1), while other constituencies, albeit factors to consider, emerged as less important.

The low ranking given other constituencies on our questionnaires may reflect just how difficult it is for them to separate concerns for the employees, customers, and so on, from the company's long-term future. However, while the majority of directors understand the conflict between their legal accountabilities to the shareholders and the company's long-term health, the ways in which they deal with such conflicts vary.

One group, a minority within a commanding majority, we call the rationalizers.

The Rationalizers

These directors see the conflicts and feel the tensions inherent in their responsibilities in an increasingly complex world. However, they rationalize them away, implicitly following the view of the Delaware courts that what's good for the shareholder will be good for other constituencies, and for the corporation.

The following comments reflect this view:

> *Relating the interests of the employees, the shareholders, the management, and so forth, is very difficult. I don't think the shareholders can be evaluated in a vacuum disregarding all of the other parties, but then again you have a legal responsibility to them. I guess I've always felt that if you do the best thing for the employee, in the long run, then, you'll be automatically doing the best thing for the shareholders.*

> *Of course, I put the interest of the shareholders in the primary position because they're the people I'm on the board to serve. Basically I believe, though, that if I'm doing what's best in the long run for the other constituencies—namely the employees, and the customers, and so forth—then I'll be doing the best thing for the shareholders at the same time. I always look at the long-term ramifications of an issue—the short-term ones are unimportant.*

Directors know their number one responsibility is to the shareholders, but to meet that effectively, they also know that the employee has to be well served. Low employee morale won't generate very high profits, and poor customer relations won't either. I think, however, that the interests of these various parties aren't in conflict; rather, I think they're in mutual consent, all working toward the same goal.

Another director disagreed:

I feel that the stockholders are definitely my first priority. I am representing them and consequently I must always have their best interests in mind when I make a decision. If the company—more specifically, the board—is fair to the stockholders, then it generally follows that we'll be fair to the employees and the community.

The Broad Constructionists

In contrast to the rationalizers, a larger, perhaps more thoughtful, group of directors openly recognizes that their responsibilities encompass more than shareholders. If this attitude produces conflicts, they recognize and deal with them, without assuming that every decision must be in the shareholders' interests. If one likens directors to Africa's magnificent ostriches, the latter group of "birds" would be actively confronting the dangers of life on the sandy plains, while the rationalizers might gaze enviously at the buried heads of the traditionalists. We call this third group the broad constructionists.

One such director, recognizing that some of his peers were rationalizing, was clear about his own thinking.

Boards were conceived to respond to the interests of the investors who elected them. Their first duty is to the stockholders, second to the employees, third to the whims of the national economy, and finally to the needs of the communities in which they operate. A director must balance the priorities and values of all of

*the above as he attempts to conform to his legal respon-
sibilities. He'd probably deny balancing the shareholders' interest with those of the other constituencies. Most
directors would claim (and thereby personally rationalize the situation) that they're incorporating the interests of the other constituencies as factors whose concerns are in the long-range interest of the firm and
thereby in the long-range interest of the stockholders.*

Another director was more explicit about his responsibility for the corporation and all its "claimants" as he described
what each expected:

> *Fundamentally, a company is an institution which
> is trying to optimize the interests of a number of com-
> peting claimants. The customer obviously wants the
> very best product at the very lowest price possible. The
> employee wants the easiest work rules and the highest
> compensation. The government wants companies to
> maintain a strong record in terms of equal opportunity
> and to get substantial exports. The shareholder clearly
> doesn't give a damn about all of that stuff; all he wants
> is to have the price of the stock soar so he can buy and
> sell and, in the meantime, get very high dividends. The
> management wants to remain intact in the position of
> power and get greater and greater rewards and better
> and better perks. The town you're operating in clearly
> wants you to pay high local taxes, hire more local
> workers, be a very good corporate citizen. . . .*
>
> *It's always a balancing act and the competing
> claims always have to be looked at realistically. You
> have to set the whole thing up so that it works. It's an
> extremely challenging undertaking and you have to be
> asking yourself constantly what changes are taking
> place among all of these competing claimants. . . . It is
> the director's job to try to balance all of these claims
> into an optimum system.*

The chairman of a major Canadian corporation, serving on
the board of a U.S. company, commented:

> *You have to consider, at all times, all of your
> stakeholders. If all of your decisions are in favor of*

your shareholders, at the expense of your consumers or your employees, you won't survive very long. Any decision has to try to put in proper perspective and balance the interest of your employees, your consumers, and your shareholders. If there are other stakeholders because of the business you're in, such as the environmentalists, you also have to put them into the equation, making sure that you are doing so within reason. You cannot give air that is 100% pure because, if you were to do that, you would have to shut the plant down. You can, however, reduce the pollution, and in so doing, you may have to ask your employees to take less of a wage increase because you will have more capital expenditures—and the shareholders will get slightly less. You have to bear in mind it's a melting pot of these various interests that must concern you at all times.

Finally, the retired CEO of one of America's largest companies described the situation that confronted his own company, and provided us with the idea of labeling those who thought as he did "broad constructionists."

Let's take the [company name] situation in 1979. The company had 510,000 employees worldwide; by 1984 we had 374,000 and we were able to produce not that much less than we were with the 510,000. Well, there's the arithmetic of the situation, and all of this added up to about $4 billion less in cost per year, to do essentially the same thing. Okay, so losing jobs and lowering costs are the hard, cold facts. But think of it, we're talking about entire communities—and we even had to go so far as to eliminate the dividend. You just cannot be unmindful of the larger responsibilities by just looking at what's in it for the shareholder, at that particular moment. So I would say that I am a broader constructionist rather than a narrower one.

The Broad Constructionist's Perspective

The majority of directors, like the retired CEO quoted above, consider themselves accountable to more stakeholders than the shareholders. Their comments illustrate their recog-

Table 3-2
Long-Term vs. Short-Term Considerations in Decisions[a]

Short-term share price	.4%
Long-term outcome for the corporation	70.3%
Balance short term and long term	26.6%
Have never encountered the dilemma	1.1%

a. Directors were asked how they resolved any conflicts between the impact of a decision on short-term stock price and long-term outcome for the corporation. "%" indicates percentage of directors responding.

nition and understanding of the corporation's importance in our society. As critical as their shareholder accountability has been historically, they believe the long-term survival of the corporations on whose boards they sit is also vital. Not surprisingly, this view is consistent with how American CEOs see their responsibilities, since almost two-thirds of the directors are current or past CEOs.[2]

These directors also realize that concern for the health of the corporation mandates a long-term perspective (see Table 3-2).

Clearly, these figures mesh with the comments quoted above. For many directors, being a board member is less simple today, as they seek to balance the long-term perspective with the conflicting traditional view of their accountabilities. The comments below reflect the complexities.

> It is your job to give an appropriate return to shareholders, but that doesn't mean you should discount the long range at any particular time. Some things will cost the shareholders money in the short term, which are essential to the long-term development and therefore are for the future benefit of the shareholders. If you don't engage in any research and development, you can save a lot of money. But then you also won't have a product at the other end of the line, your competition will gobble you up, and you won't have a company. One must always sort out what is the short-term view and what is the longer-term view for the growth and the health of

2. Gordon Donaldson and Jay W. Lorsch, *Decision Making at the Top* (New York: Basic Books, 1983), p. 30.

*the company, which means that you have to have a
sharper, longer-range view if you are sensible. The
shareholders as a whole will be better off, in your best
judgment, than they would have been if you got thrifty
on the wrong thing.*

*It's not always easy because it might enhance
shareholder value to sell a particular division or an as-
set or something like that. But then you have to look at
the synergies that exist within the company and you
have to decide, well, instead of selling this off and enhancing the immediate value to the shareholders, is it
better to put more research and more capital into it and
hope that in the long run, it will yield a higher return
for the company?*

*There are times when you just have to concentrate
on the potential for profit in two or three years. It might
lead to decisions that would look ill-advised in a snap-
shot. . . . "Sustaining" is a good word. It is important
to have profits sustained over a five-year period. You
make a long-term investment in the company, and in
the United States, even though it may not be as profitable as you would like for several years.*

This strong commitment to the long term also refutes the
popular criticism that U.S. business leaders are too short-term-
oriented.[3] Strangely, though, as committed as they are to the
premise that long-term company health is an appropriate objective and will ultimately benefit the shareholders, most directors are still uneasy about going against the narrower traditional view of shareholder primacy. In other words, even as
they act in the way they believe is most responsible, they are
unable to do so without qualms. The courts, in dealing with,
for example, takeover cases, do tend to adopt a short-term
view of shareholder benefit, a perspective that may reinforce
the uneasiness many directors feel.

The trend away from individual shareholders to institu-

---

3. Again, this long-term perspective is consistent with the fact that as an earlier
   study revealed, U.S. CEOs are more concerned with the long term than their
   critics have suggested. Ibid.

tions is, of course, another reason why directors are increasingly adopting a long-term view, fearing the potential danger of feeding the voracious appetite of today's "take-the-money-and-run" shareholders. One CEO-director described his view of the conflict:

> The real conflict of interest occurs between the short-term stock price interests of those who own shares of stock on a given day and whose attitude toward value reflects a desire to get the most value for the stock that day, and, on the other hand, the constituencies whose interests are more long-term, which would include employees who want a job tomorrow, next month, and next year, or investors whose personal situations cause them to be less interested in the value of the share that day and more interested in the total value of the enterprise as a long-term investment. I think the question of just whom does a director represent and how does he deal with the apparent conflicts I've described is without an abstract solution.

Another director reflected the tension many felt between short-term pressures for shareholder gain and their understanding of the actions and time necessary to improve a company's financial results:

> Management should not be perpetuated unconditionally but, on the other hand, it shouldn't be subject to being put on the block because some investment banking firm wants to make a quick buck and because the stock is underpriced. If the stock is underpriced, (a) I want my management to be able to work to get the price up to its full value, and (b) I'd like that value to go to the shareholders and not to the guy who buys it at some point between the current price and the full price.

By shareholders, this director means the loyal investor who holds the company's shares for the long term and, from the perspective of the directors, institutions are the least loyal shareholders. In fact, they have difficulty taking the institutional owner seriously, believing its goals are at odds with the corporation's longer-term interests and are too concerned with short-term gain. A director spoke for many of his peers:

> One thing that substantially muddies the water about this so called constituency-governance problem is that more and more people are coming to the realization that the shareholders are really a bunch of 26-year-olds sitting behind their trading desks, and that the people who have the best interest of the company and its employees at heart are really those in management. . . . The big companies are now institutionally held in a major proportion, so when you look at your shareholder list for the last six months, the shareholders are all brand-new. Then you have the hostile raider in there saying, "Well, I'm representing the shareholder." The directors and management, like at Phillips Petroleum, are left saying, "There's no company here anymore—all these people are out of work and the company has been fragmented." So who benefited in all of this? A very limited number of people who maybe two years before had had no knowledge that that company existed. This is causing a whole lot of new difficulty in directors' minds—just where is the best interest of the company? Especially if you complicate the debate with the question: Are you talking about tomorrow or are you talking about ten years from now? Yeah, we can see a run up on the stock for a limited period of time right now, and maybe you take the profit from that. Then the traders get out and there's only debris left because maybe the company had uglied itself with some type of a recapitalization plan or a poison pill to try to ward off the unfriendly takeover. So these are all the new currents that make directorships the job that nobody wants.

For many directors, the broad-constructionist view makes more sense than trying to represent shareholders, whose short-term goals conflict with their view of what's best for the company and the country. The perspective bubbles over into clear hostility in the minds of many, like the director just quoted, toward the arbitrageurs and other short-term investors.

Another director had these questions: "Even with regard

to investors there is a question as to whether there is really a
responsible investor, and who is that investor? Can an arbi-
trageur be a responsible investor?''

A third director had equally strong views.

> Of all the changes that have occurred and the prob-
> lems that exist, I think the most pressing issue that now
> confronts corporate directors is this question of who are
> the constituencies they represent. With all of this cops-
> and-robbers merger mania, the only winners are the ar-
> bitrageurs—not the stockholders, and certainly not the
> old-type, long-term stockholders. I think it's very sad
> the way upstanding, credible firms are being tossed
> around and broken up like heads of cauliflower. . . .

A final comment combines several reasons why so many
directors have taken a broader view of their accountabilities.

> First off, I would say we have the shareholders, but
> who are they? Some companies have 60% to 70% in-
> stitutional investors. Here you are deciding what's right
> for the shareholders, the employees, the community,
> and the whole thing. For example, if the company is
> the largest employer in a particular town and it decides
> to shut down the main plant, then I submit that a direc-
> tor has to pay some attention to that.
>
> But coming back to the shareholders, it was a lot
> easier when 90% of the shareholders were individuals
> and you could say we have the widows in Iowa to con-
> sider for the long haul. We would plan for their staying
> with us for two or three years down the road, if not de-
> cades, but now we have a shareholder who's with you
> on a Tuesday and on a Wednesday he's gone and then
> he's back again on a Friday. How do you attend to his
> interests? This is a terrible problem for directors as they
> attempt to take the long-term view. If anything comes
> up that would worsen the share price, then many direc-
> tors would vote against it. For example, if a firm takes
> on a new research project, then the pension fund man-
> agers will sell your shares, and your share price will
> decline even though the project may be an essential

move to put you in a stronger competitive position for the future, and may also be in the shareholders' best interests. This careful attention to quarterly earnings and the short-term view may severely hurt our competitive position vis-à-vis the Japanese, who have always claimed we take the wrong approach.

Charade in the Boardroom

Thus we found the majority of directors felt trapped in a dilemma between their traditional legal responsibility to shareholders, whom they consider too interested in short-term payout, and beliefs about what is best, in the long run, for the health of the company. For most, the broad view makes more sense. Some, of course, rationalize that taking account of other constituencies is always in the interest of the shareholder, while a minority adhere to the traditional legal view of accountability only to shareholders.

In a typical boardroom, then, we can imagine several factions, each thinking differently about the board's purposes. This alone could impede the decision-making process, but the situation is further complicated by directors' reluctance to discuss their purposes beyond the traditional salute to shareholder interests. For traditionalists and rationalizers alike, there is no reason to question their purpose. Both are wedded to the narrow issue of shareholder interest. But every broad constructionist considers criteria other than short-term shareholder value, though he or she does not talk about it with colleagues. As a result, board discussions, like the example at the outset of this chapter, often resemble a charade where directors, working toward the corporation's long-term interests, avoid revealing their standards and criteria or their deep belief in the need for a broad perspective. Without a shared, explicit understanding of its purpose, the board's capacity for coherent discussion and its power as a group are impaired. The situation is especially complicated because management, on the other hand, is likely to be very clear about its goals. The should-be, would-be governors too often are powerless against the clearly articulated unity of those they are meant to govern.

Their legal mandate often means little in the complex reality
of governance.

The Evolving Legal Context

An obvious question is, Why don't directors discuss the
board's true purpose? It appears that, in many boards, a group
norm has evolved prohibiting such discussion.[4] The core of
the inhibition is the widely held view that directors' legal
responsibility is solely to shareholders. If directors believe
this, discussing other accountabilities seems unnecessary and,
if not illegal, at least inappropriate.

The vast majority of directors seem unaware that the legal
context defining their accountability is changing, both ap-
ropos of the normal conduct of corporate affairs and in relation to directors' actions in considering a sale of the company.
The most obvious source of change is innovation in the laws of
the seventeen states "which permit directors to consider the
interests of constituents other than the corporation's shareholders." In these jurisdictions (again, excluding Delaware),
directors have no legal reason to feel inhibited in discussing
their broader purposes. However, they may find it difficult to
understand and use their broader powers, since stipulations
about how to assess the interests of various stakeholders are
unclear in many of these laws. Further, the courts' interpretation of specific laws is still evolving.[5]

Nonetheless, court decisions in many jurisdictions, including Delaware, are clear on one broad point—directors
do have the right to consider stakeholders other than shareholders.

An eminent corporate lawyer explained:

When you come to the communities and the em-
ployees, I think the courts are very clear. The directors

---

4. Chris Argyris provides a comprehensive discussion of such behavior in *Strategy
   Change and Defensive Routines* (Boston: Pitman, 1985).
5. James A. Hanks, "Recent Legislation on D&O Liability Limitation," *The Business
   Lawyer* (August 1988), p. 1227.

> have the right to consider those [constituencies], pro-
> vided the directors are not in the business of selling the
> corporation. If they are going to run the company, then
> they have to be good citizens, because it's good for the
> shareholders, in some cosmic way, and it's good for
> society.

Thus, in the conduct of normal business affairs, directors have
the latitude to consider constituencies other than shareholders. As pointed out above, this opinion is consistent with the
traditional interpretation of Delaware law.

Even in times of crisis, they are not as constrained by
the law as many seem to believe. In states without the broadened law, directors must consider the question of sale from
the shareholders' perspective, but this doesn't mean that they
must automatically accept the offer that benefits the shareholders most in the short term.

The courts' first concern is the process by which the board
reached its decision because of "the duty of care." As a lawyer
explained:

> [In] the cases where selling the company has come
> up, the court will look at the objectiveness of the way
> you've gone about the process. The most objective of all
> is if the offer is all in cash. When somebody is offering
> you paper and somebody else is offering you less in
> cash, then how do you evaluate the long-term value of
> the paper? You get into entirely different circumstances.
> You also get into all sorts of circumstances based on
> how you run the auction, whether it is a sealed-bid auc-
> tion or an open auction or both. We've had courts bless
> taking a lower number, where there was a certainty of
> financing, against the higher number, where there was
> no certainty of financing. The procedures are very im-
> portant in terms of the way you run the auction, and
> that itself can result in huge price differentials, despite
> what you would normally expect would be the result.

Even more fundamentally, the courts have ruled consistently that the business judgment rule does apply to such decisions. So there is no reason for a board to believe it must

automatically sell the company to the highest bidder. Our legal authority went on:

> A board of directors will never be liable for refus-
> ing to sell the company. The issue arose several years
> ago where the directors were interested parties who
> would lose their jobs if the company was sold. The
> question was, Did the business judgment rule apply in
> such a case? The Seventh, the First, and the Second cir-
> cuit courts all passed on it and said that every director,
> in every situation, wants to stay in office. Selling the
> company doesn't alter that fact and, therefore, the busi-
> ness judgment rule still applies.
>
> The decision to sell a company is considered by
> the board very seriously these days—and they try to
> figure out if they must sell. In each of the cases I men-
> tioned, where this came up, the stock had gone way
> down. In one case they had turned down a $40 per
> share offer and the stock was selling at $17 when the
> court made the decision, but that's life—you can't be
> looking at this stuff in hindsight. What I hear a lot of
> people saying is that you have to go to an investment
> bank in these sorts of situations and have them say
> whether or not it's fair, but that's not the issue. The
> question is whether you have to sell the company.
>
> I always tell the directors, "I don't care what the
> investment bankers tell you—you have a right to make
> your own judgment on what you think the future course
> of the world will be. If you think interest rates are going
> to go up 2% and therefore the company is going to be
> worth a lot more, you may be wrong—but it's your
> judgment and that's what you have to act on. But if it's
> totally off the wall, and no reasonable man would even
> think about it, then a court may second-guess you . . . if
> you think the long-term future of the company is such
> that you don't want to sell it even though it's a fair
> offer, then you don't have to."

Thus, what directors are legally required to do both in normal times and when the company is under attack is less in conflict with their own concern for the company's survival than many believe. The confusion abounding in this arena is illustrated by the attention *The Wall Street Journal* gave to a memorandum Martin Lipton, the well-known partner in the law firm of Wachtell, Lipton, Rosen and Katz, wrote to his clients.[6] Mr. Lipton's point was similar to ours. That *The Wall Street Journal* found it newsworthy may be an independent measure of the current misconceptions.

This discussion also raises another important issue. If we now accept that directors have broader accountabilities and that many shareholders have no long-term interest in a particular corporation, then the shareholder right to elect directors becomes questionable. Add to these changes, the shareholders' actual lack of participation in choosing directors (as described in Chapter 2) and it may be time now to discuss the unthinkable—whether shareholders *should* have the right to elect directors. We hope that our research will stimulate such a debate, and we shall return to this matter in the final chapter.

Conclusions

America's public corporations are critical to the national well-being and must be governed from that perspective. This fact requires a concern for long-term survival: a concern that often goes beyond the singular interest of shareholders, as presently constituted.[7] Big changes are taking place that must be understood and addressed. Beyond the continuing vital importance of corporations, both the commanding position of institutional investors and the evolving, but broader, legal parameters mean that directors can and must look beyond their traditional shareholder accountability.

Obviously, directors must be better informed of their legal responsibilities if they are to provide sound governance. If they are, they will be able to develop an explicit, shared

---

6. *The Wall Street Journal*, Eastern edition, November 4, 1988, p. B5.
7. James O'Toole, in *Vanguard Management: Redesigning the Corporate Future* (New York: Doubleday, 1985), has gone so far as to assert that companies that demonstrate a concern for all constituencies also have the strongest performance. A similar point was made by James Burke, chairman and CEO of Johnson & Johnson in a speech to the Harvard Business School Club of Greater New York, when he was given the Business Statesman Award, March 30, 1987.

understanding of their objectives, and this would be an important step in enhancing the outside directors' collective ability to govern.

From what we have learned, the majority of today's directors already share, in spirit, the broader charge given them by modern law. They just don't realize that their desire to uphold the long-term interests of the corporation and of various stakeholders puts them on the right side of their legal obligations.

Chapter 4

The Board at Work: Normalcy

No one, other than the directors, the CEO-chairman, and the corporate secretary, knows what transpires behind the closed doors of the corporate boardroom. As we saw in Chapter 1, the traditional legal perspective has defined the directors' duties: overseeing and evaluating management and the performance of the corporation, reviewing and approving major corporate plans and actions, and assuring that corporate actions are ethical, socially responsible, and within the law. However, such lists are merely skeletons of the diverse functions directors might perform. In actuality, each board develops its own interpretation of how to carry out its legal mandate, although we shall present some common trends. Further, such lists ignore the complexities and subtleties of the relationships between the power of management and that of directors.

In this chapter and the next, we enter the nation's boardrooms to learn how directors normally carry out their legal authority, how they prepare for meetings, and what takes place in terms of both content and process.

Meeting Preparation

Outside directors are part-timers, for whom board meetings are episodic events, whether they occur monthly or, more typically, five to nine times a year. Before each meeting, directors, who must reconnect with the issues facing that particular company, review the information provided in advance.

Information

While the amount and timing of information sent to board members varies, directors reported that most corporations provided similar information (see Table 4-1).

Table 4-1
Information Received in Advance of Meetings

(Scale: 1 = Always Receive 5 = Never Receive)	
Minutes of prior meetings	1.17
Agenda of future meetings	1.31
Financial statements	1.37
Specific management proposals	1.98
Committee reports	2.17

Directors customarily receive prior minutes and agendas before the next meeting. Whatever the legal and procedural purposes of the material, it enables them to reinvolve themselves in the company's affairs. We stress this fact because, in normal times, directors have little need to be involved with the company between meetings and may benefit from memory jogging.

More important are the financial statements, the review of which provides an opportunity to prepare questions and comments. Management proposals and committee reports, although provided less frequently, give board members a more thorough knowledge of the issues up for discussion. Although some directors feel they don't receive enough substantive information, or that they don't have it sufficiently in advance, most are satisfied. One director's comments were typical.

> *I think that directors are more aware of what is going on in the companies where they serve, and the decisions they make are based upon much better information. This is an essential change because the world, not only the business community, is far more complex than it has ever been before, and it's essential that the individuals guiding the major enterprises are up-to-date and well informed.*

A second director believed, as did most of his peers, that more information, if needed, was readily available: "What I have seen on this and other boards, including my own, is that management is much more open. On almost any board, anybody can request any information and, if one person doesn't ask for it, someone else will."

Though directors are positive about the availability of information, they still have a problem in interpreting and using it, because the data required to comprehend issues such as past corporate performance, management's proposals, or long-term strategy are often complex and predicated on a detailed knowledge of the company and its businesses. For example, if directors are asked to approve a major capital expenditure for a new plant that will manufacture a new product, they need data on sales volume, costs, return on investments, and so on. While management provides such data, the forecasts are predicated on assumptions and judgments about customer needs and responses, the performance of workers and machinery, and fluctuations in the marketplace. Generally, experienced people in a particular industry can evaluate or challenge the estimates and assumptions. Even though most directors are highly talented and experienced, they're rarely familiar enough with a particular business to assess such proposals properly. This complexity has inspired a few directors to call for an independent staff for the board. For example:

> One thing that I think ought to change is the fact that boards don't have permanent staffs to assist them. They need some sort of mechanism to help them delve deeper into the problems that corporations confront. The committees are not enough. In fact, they need some assistance from some sort of staff, as well.

This isn't a new idea. It was part of a plan, suggested in 1972, by former justice Arthur Goldberg when he was on the board of Trans World Airlines, that proposed forming a committee of directors to function separately from the executive committee.[1] He envisaged it overseeing company operations on a broad scale and making periodic reports to the en-

---

1. Donald E. Schwartz, "A Plan to Save the Board," *The Record of the Association of the Bar of the City of New York 28* (April 1973): 279–289.

tire board, and proposed that the committee be empowered to hire an independent staff of experts, responsible only to the board. His list is informative: a scientific adviser to examine product-line developments, an economist to investigate future markets, a public-relations expert, an independent auditor, and, perhaps, a financial expert. The suggested variety illustrates the complex range of issues facing directors, but when he submitted his proposal to the TWA management, it created a furor inside and outside the company. The proposal was turned down and he resigned from the board.

Since the idea of having a separate staff was so soundly rejected then, and seems unlikely to be more positively received today, the directors' lack of in-depth knowledge and judgment of complex information remains a problem. Often, they must decide about complicated matters with scant understanding of the underlying assumptions and factors that will affect the outcome, and with inadequate preparation time to more fully grasp the issues at hand. In addition, the limited discussion time during board meetings restricts their understanding as well as their ability to contribute to decisions. So, while directors are obtaining better information, problems in understanding and utilizing it critically limit the exercise of their legal power.

One remedy to the lack of directors' time has been an increase in the number of board committees, which, it is generally agreed, facilitates the work of directors. By 1987, 75% of the boards of industrial companies had 3 to 5 committees, the most common of which were audit, compensation, and nominating. Other prevalent committees are finance and pension-retirement. More interesting from our perspective is the emergence of strategic planning committees, which, while among the least prevalent, are now included in 44.2% of the Fortune 1000 boards.[2]

Committee Meetings

Beyond doing their best to digest the information before a board meeting, directors also prepare for board meetings by participating in committee meetings.

2. Heidrick & Struggles, The Changing Board, p. 5.

Several directors articulated their colleagues' views.

Without a doubt, committees are crucial. If the whole board dwelt on every issue that the compensation or the audit committee considers, we wouldn't have time to hold down jobs elsewhere. The audit committee gets a hell of a lot done, and I'd say I spend as much time concentrating on audit problems as I do dwelling on the problems of the company as a whole.

As long as I have been a director, most of the work that has gone on is in committees—the close working with operating executives and the preparation and development of an analysis, plus recommendations as to what to do, staff support for it, along with preparation to deal with future questions as to why you did not do something else—all that goes on in committees. You can't have 12 to 15 people working as carefully as they must through issues that come to the board, so you have to divide the work load among the members.

In my experience, I have observed that the work of the board is done in committees, because some of it requires specific knowledge, and more time than board members might be able to give to all of the subjects a board will consider. Therefore, you are asked to concentrate on specific areas and other board members, then rely on each other—to the extent that each board member determines what's sufficient to represent his interest and the interests he's there to serve. He has to rely on the presentations of other board members on the committees considering the specific and detailed subjects that the company confronts.

Clearly, committees enable directors to cope with two of the most important problems they face—the limited time they have available, and the complexity of the information with which they must deal.

Audit and compensation committees, where the information and issues are complicated and detailed, are particularly helpful. But, as we mentioned in Chapter 2, the nominating committee's role can be complicated by the CEO's involvement in nominating directors.

For the committees to function well, directors have to trust each other enough to let a subgroup decide matters for all of them. From our discussions with directors, we find the system works better with audit and compensation committees than with strategic planning committees, where the directors are less sanguine about trusting a subgroup. Because strategic planning is so vital, some fear that relegating it to a committee might reduce the involvement of other directors. The issue, however, is more one of wanting to be involved than of lacking confidence in other board members.

The Board Meeting

After preparing individually and in committees, directors and members of senior management in many companies meet and chat informally at a dinner the night before the board meeting. The gatherings have a purpose, which will become evident as we describe a typical board meeting. As the directors assemble the next morning, in many boards they find the seating arrangement is preordained, with the chairman at the head of the table and directors seated by seniority, so that the most recently elected members are farthest from the chairman.

The Agenda

While specific agendas differ, our interviews reveal a basic pattern to most meetings. One director's description follows.

> A typical meeting begins with the management bringing the directors up to speed as to what has happened over the past month, in terms of the company's financial situation, what the earnings have been, and so forth. You then get an update on the prospects for the future. Then, most important, the directors are brought up to speed as to the other factors that may affect the company: information about a merger or an acquisition that may be going on, or anything that may affect

public or employee safety. We also discuss broader is-
sues such as South Africa, currency changes, or tax re-
form, and determine how they may affect operations.
These are the regular agenda items, and then every
quarter we declare a dividend.

Another director says:

The first matter of business is routine—the review
of the minutes of the previous meeting. Most of the time
the next topic is an update on current operations or
those related to financial matters, marketing, and so
forth. Then there are the reports of the various commit-
tees and, after that, the board receives new information.
Examples are major contracts the company may enter
into, acquisitions or spin-offs, and dividend payments.
Then the board discusses any litigation and, finally,
any other miscellaneous issues that may have come up.
This seems to be a typical board meeting, and they run
anywhere from one hour to seven, depending on the is-
sues being discussed.

Directors consider the "Report of the CEO" the most important event of a normal meeting. It's also the most time-
consuming, with the CEO informing the directors about what
is going on at the company and describing his plans for the
future (see Table 4-2). His report often includes assessments of

Table 4-2
Agenda Items

	Importance 1 = Very important 5 = Not important	Time Spent 1 = A great deal 5 = Next to none
Report of the CEO	1.37	1.92
Specific management proposals	1.50	1.72
Past financial results	1.68	2.08
Potential ownership changes	1.75	2.88
Capital allocation decisions	1.94	2.38
Committee reports	2.19	3.04
Legal issues	2.26	2.77
Approval of minutes	3.90	4.73

the firm's financial performance, results of various divisions, changes in management, and an update of the events since the previous meeting.

Specific management proposals are next in importance and are given ample discussion time. Top managers, who report to the CEO, generally present the proposals, then it's the directors' turn to ask questions and offer suggestions.

Reviewing past financial results is the third most important and time-consuming activity, giving directors an opportunity to scrutinize the company's overall performance, as well as its various businesses. This report generally includes budget forecasts, which enable directors to consider probable future financial results. On many boards, the presentation, distinct from the CEO's report, is given by the chief financial officer and the controller and contains more financial detail than the CEO's overview.

Although capital allocation decisions rank next in terms of time, they're less important than "potential changes in ownership." Obviously, changes of ownership are not normal events, and we shall discuss them in Chapter 6 as crises, but when they do occur, they get the directors' attention. Questions of capital allocation are usually closely connected to specific management proposals, and often immediately follow the presentation by the managers involved. In approving money for a specific project, directors essentially are endorsing management's plans.

While directors praise the work of the committees, the committee reports to the board are almost a formality, and little time is devoted to them, suggesting that directors do trust their colleagues to have considered properly the issue in question.

Finally, legal issues ranked next-to-last in importance, but are the fifth most time-consuming activity, because boards are legally required to address many specific matters that are, from the directors' point of view, routine: for example, the annual election of officers, which is simply the confirmation of the status quo, or the appointment of auditors, which is usually the continuation of a long-standing relationship with a respected public accounting firm, and a confirmation of the audit committee decision. Other legal activity—for instance, a report on litigation involving the board—is usually presented by the corporate counsel.

While traditional and legal requirements have had an impact on board meeting agendas, in terms of the sequence of issues discussed and the types of decisions made, the way directors evaluate the time needed for and the importance of a specific item is shaped more by their own perceptions of their role. As the meeting is winding down, while the directors restlessly check their watches and turn their thoughts to travel arrangements and other engagements, we will slip out of the boardroom and turn our attention to the directors' view of the function they serve in a normal board meeting.

The Directors' Real Job

With no precise legal definition of what directors must do to govern, their actual duties have been worked out in each boardroom. Yet directors share a strong consensus about their duties under normal conditions. Organizations like the American Bar Association, the American Management Association, and the Business Roundtable may have contributed to the consensus with suggestions about directors' duties, and by creating a climate in which directors want to make their jobs more meaningful. But the emergent consensus reflects certain aspects of the common reality directors face. They must "manage" within their legal mandate, without usurping the duties of the corporation's top managers. Thus, their job concept has evolved out of the reality of what they *could* do, given their time, knowledge, and real power compared to that of the CEO and other top managers. The parameters, apparently, vary little across companies, leading to a common view.

The consensus forged by these forces identifies three major duties: selecting, assessing, rewarding, and, if necessary, replacing the CEO; determining strategic direction; and assuring ethical and legal conduct. We'll examine each activity and relate it to the matters discussed in a typical board meeting—the forum in which almost all normal work is done.

Care and Feeding of the CEO

Of their three duties, directors believe the most critical one is what we call the care and feeding of the chief executive officer. Two directors had this typical view:

> The real determinant of the success or failure of a corporation is the CEO. I have to stress again that a director's job is picking the CEO and getting rid of him if he doesn't prove he is qualified. It is one of the hardest tasks any individual will ever face, but the stakes are extremely high.

> I guess the most important role that the board plays is selecting the CEO. It doesn't happen very often, so it isn't a regular responsibility, but it's a very important one. The board doesn't run the company, but it has to make sure that the people who do are the best that are available.

A third director felt a director's role was severely limited:

> You only have two actions. One is deciding when to fire the CEO and who the replacement will be. You don't use that action loosely, though, because, by and large, good CEOs are hard to come by and you just don't turn them away unless you really feel you can do better and have to do better. The second action is setting his salary and his bonus.

While most directors believe their main responsibility is to hire and fire the CEO, it's one they rarely exercise. Thus, despite its importance, it occupies little of their time under normal conditions. Directors spend much more time advising the CEO, a task that, while not as dramatic as replacing him, enables them to play what many consider to be their key normal duty. Two directors described the board's role as counselors:

> I would say that the role of a director is to keep extremely well informed and just advise the management to the best of his ability. He can't do much more than that.

Directors are sounding boards for management.
They contribute their opinions as to general policy, and
their judgment whenever a problem comes up.

When directors refer to this duty, they first describe their responsibilities in relation to the CEO, and for some, the duty may end there, but most directors have a broader concern with top management in general.

The view of themselves as counselors to the CEO, as well as other top managers, stems from the traditional legal definition of the director's job. A director explained: "If you read the bylaws of the corporation, they read as if the board is proactive in managing the business. The bylaws talk about managing the affairs of the company, but, as a matter of fact, it is not what happens and is not what should happen. What the board should do is watch and counsel the management."

Directors use several features of the typical board meeting to carry out their activities, but the "Report of the CEO" gives them the best opportunity to understand the CEO's thinking about past events and future plans, and to build a data base of accumulated knowledge. If things are proceeding well, individual directors generally store the knowledge without discussing it. When problems arise, as we shall explain in subsequent chapters, directors may begin to share both knowledge and perceptions.

In a few companies, however, a more formal evaluation of the CEO's performance takes place, either by the full board or by a committee. However, from our data, formal and explicit reviews are the rare exceptions, regrettably, since such reviews are one way directors can constructively clarify their legal power vis-à-vis the CEO.

Assessing the capabilities of top managers who are subordinate to the CEO is an ongoing task during normal board meetings. As these managers make presentations to the board, directors have a chance to see how they perform on their feet, how they react to questions, and how they think. Companies that have dinners prior to the board meeting justify them as an opportunity for directors to meet informally with managers. In fact, such events are almost the only times when outside directors interact informally with top managers.

Finally, the compensation committee in most companies is also involved in assessing top management, especially on matters related to rewards and potential successors. Again, the committees vary in how well, and to what extent, they carry out their duties. However, their mere existence bodes well for the board's increased, explicit, and more proactive involvement in the company.

Determining Strategic Direction

Many directors also define the boundary between their duties and those of management by combining their roles as evaluators of and counselors to the CEO, with an involvement in corporate strategic planning. A director described the fine line between the duties of directors and managers.

> Basically, directors have to make the major decisions; they have to come to grips with the issue of where the company should be going. For example, should the company be borrowing a lot of money as a matter of policy and leveraging itself, as opposed to contracting and not leveraging itself? Should the company go into a new line of business? Those are decisions made at the board level, but there is a very fine line between what the board does and what the CEO does.

The combination of strategic planning and assessing and counseling the CEO works best when the corporation is doing well. But dissatisfied directors are rarely openly critical, as we shall explain in Chapter 5. They must influence events in much subtler ways, as they assess managers' presentations and plans. Our interviews revealed that an increasing number of directors linked their roles as advisers and counselors to their strategic involvement. For example:

> Directors should choose the CEO and support him until he proves unworthy. They should assist in financial planning and strategic decision making, as well as provide advice when the company decides it wants to leave its normal business area.

A director's key roles are evaluating the CEO and the company's performance, overseeing management development, and making certain that the future strategy the company is developing focuses on the firm's strengths, so that it will be competitive in the international markets.

While most directors stress the connection between strategy formulation and their role as advisers and evaluators, some consider their involvement in strategic discussions paramount. One director explained:

Directors are an important part of the policy/direction of the companies on whose boards they serve. A few directors have an awful lot to do not just with the ceremonial decisions, but also with sorting out what to do in the running of a large firm. I don't know that that act is broadly appreciated. The fiduciary role, the making sure that the management in place doesn't screw up, tends to be overglamorized, and the thinking through of where the company is going is underemphasized among directors' roles.

Another director elaborated:

An important function of the board is determining what general policies the firm will attempt to carry out. They have to decide such things as: Are we going to make a particular company a conglomerate? Are we going to have one that is motivated by the bottom line or by our research and development? Are we going to expand in a small market or are we going to become international? These are all policy questions that have to be answered by management, but recommended to the board for their final approval, so the board has the ultimate say as to the direction the company will take.

Finally, a director articulated a view, held by many, that in today's dynamic world, the board needs to be more involved in strategic matters.

I think forward planning is a part of the board's responsibility, particularly in today's climate. Perhaps 10 *to 15 years ago that wasn't too important. You did the same thing over and over again; you did it well and the market would take care of it. That, however, is no longer the case. Now, if you don't know what new projects are in the works and how they're being developed, you really aren't in much of a position to be very critical. I think a strategic planning committee is critical, and the plans it devises should be reviewed with the full board so that it will have an opportunity to provide input.*

This director was one who believed that, in addition to full-board participation in strategic planning, every board should have a strategic planning committee. While these committees are still controversial, a few years ago the thought of the board's involvement in strategic planning, or of a strategic planning committee, was even more controversial. Things have changed dramatically since the early 1980s. For example, in a tongue-in-cheek paper written in 1984, Thomas Whisler stated the "rules of the game" for directors.[3] One rule was "We [directors] don't set strategy." Whisler goes on to explain that the board should cast a "critical eye" on strategy and "bear the responsibility for insisting that the CEO develop sound and explicit strategy for the company. . . . "

Kenneth R. Andrews has argued vigorously for more board involvement in strategy formulation, and his several *Harvard Business Review* articles, in the early 1980s, drew heated criticism from many CEOs and others, who felt the board's involvement in strategy formulation would usurp prerogatives reserved for management.[4] Although the traditional legal perspective was invoked to protect management rights, Andrews recognized that the critical uproar was related to the question of CEO power. In response to criticism about his proposal for strategic planning committees, he stated:

3. Thomas J. Whisler, "Rules of the Game: Inside the Board Room," selected papers, University of Chicago Graduate School of Business, October 1987, based on a book of the same name published by Dow Jones–Irwin in 1984.

4. See, for example, Kenneth R. Andrews, "Corporate Strategy as a Vital Function of the Board," *Harvard Business Review* (November–December 1981), pp. 174–184 or "Directors' Responsibilities for Corporate Strategy," *Harvard Business Review* (November–December 1980), pp. 30–42.

> *As I say amen to all this, I have the unworthy sus-*
> *picion that I have been defeated by the most sophis-*
> *ticated put-down of all. That is, the chief executive who*
> *does not really want his board to delve deeply into stra-*
> *tegic questions—for whatever reason—will keep strat-*
> *egy out of the hands of a specially qualified and infor-*
> *mal committee.*[5]

Because of the increasingly complex problems U.S. companies are facing, both domestically and internationally, pressure to form strategic planning committees and for more board involvement in strategic questions has increased. While this type is still one of the least prevalent board committees, the fact that almost one-half of the *Fortune* 1000 firms have them is additional evidence of directors' growing involvement in strategic matters. A number of directors addressed the issue and the two following quotations express the view of many.

> *The times have been so dynamic and things have*
> *been changing so rapidly that the directors' involve-*
> *ment in the strategies of the business is greater than it*
> *has ever been.*

> *One of the major benefits of all of the recent up-*
> *heavals in corporate America, over the past decade, is*
> *that there has been a heightened sensitivity on the part*
> *of directors as to exactly what their responsibilities are*
> *in terms of planning for the future.*

Whether the whole board addresses strategic issues in plenary sessions, or with the support of a strategic planning committee, more boards are staking out a role in this arena. In fact, in a small but growing number of companies, the board has an extended meeting of a full day or two days annually to review and discuss corporate strategy, providing outside directors with more time and information to consider complex matters. But, even with such positive steps, directors still deal with strategic issues in the context of limited time and information. To us, this is a reality that cannot be ignored, even as we applaud the efforts progressive boards are making to ameliorate the difficulties.

5. Andrews, "Corporate Strategy as a Vital Function of the Board," p. 182.

Doing the Right Thing

The cluster of duties involving the CEO and the more recent emphasis on involvement in corporate strategy are the duties most stressed by directors. However, they agree, there is a third, less talked-of, area of responsibility—assuring that the corporation's affairs are conducted in an ethical, legal, and socially responsible fashion. In essence, directors believe that part of their job is to ensure that managers are doing the right thing. These issues clearly demonstrate the inherent conflicts that can arise between the narrow definition of accountability to shareholders, and the broad-constructionist's view. One director took the extreme position that management should concern itself with short-term financial results, while the board took the longer-term broader view.

> When a director makes a decision, he has to think very carefully about how the public will perceive the impact of the decision. The members of top management have to be sure to worry about how something will affect quarterly results, but it is up to the directors to consider the overall image of the firm.

But most board members would agree with the director who said: "You have to consider what kinds of policies you are going to institute in order to be a good citizen at the same time you are making the business run, so there are, in fact, many constituencies."

A concrete example was provided by a retired CEO, as he described his own company's history of investment in South Africa.

> We lost money down there year after year while, at the same time, we were spending thousands on the uplift program for the blacks. How can you argue that it's good for the shareholders? There it is, right on the table. We were losing money year after year, but we say, "Well, we've been there for the last fifty years and we have a responsibility"—and then you introduce the social aspect and the political pressures. I guess the

only way to respond to this is with what Harry Truman said, "If you can't stand the heat, get out of the kitchen." But that's the role of being a director of an international company.

There was some disagreement about why ethical and legal questions were being encountered more frequently. A few directors argued that changing board composition was responsible.

I think that the composition of American boards has changed significantly over the last 10 years or so. The discipline represented and the areas of expertise are far more varied than they were a decade ago, when boards were composed almost entirely of CEOs and lawyers. Now there are women, minorities, academics, and professionals serving on today's boards, bringing with them many diverse perspectives and insights. I think this change has done a great deal to make corporate America far more open-minded and socially conscious—both changes for the better.

The majority of directors suggest another reason. A director who was also an academic explained: "Well, I think in some sense society is demanding that business be more responsible, and this new demand is showing up not only in the behavior of management, but of boards. They're saying, 'Let's reach a position that makes some sense both as corporate citizens, and as profit-making enterprises.' "

Regardless of the factors behind the changes, that they have occurred is not debatable. Directors firmly believe that ensuring company management complies with ethical, legal, and social standards is an important part of their job. Two specific board activities deal with such matters. The first, obviously, is when the directors discuss legal matters. The second is the work of the audit committee, since one of its purposes is to ensure that there are no accounting malpractices or fraud. But, more generally, the majority of directors, especially those who accept the broad-constructionist view of accountability, believe these issues pertain to most aspects of their work in the boardroom.

The Director's Contribution

Beyond role definitions and job descriptions, we wondered how valuable directors considered their board meeting contributions (see Table 4-3). Though only 12.3% chose the highest category, close to 50% rated their contributions in the next highest category. More than one-third, however, chose the lower three categories.

Table 4-3
Director Contribution at Meetings

(Scale: 1 = A Great Deal	5 = Very Little)
1	12.3%
2	49.6%
3	32.5%
4	5.1%
5	.5%

It may be good news that so many directors believe they're making a difference, but with a sizable minority viewing their contributions as, in varying degrees, less significant, there's obviously room for improvement in the corporate governance system. If there is evidence that some directors rate their contributions outside the regular meetings as more important, we found no sign of it, despite the fact that 57% reported at least monthly contact with the CEO.

Not surprisingly, directors who have outside contact view its significance differently. One director gave a rationale:

> I think the CEO's contact with the board is beneficial, especially when difficult problems are coming up. The directors should definitely be a sounding board, both individually and collectively, for management. That can only be accomplished by a CEO who talks to his board outside of the board meeting. He calls them up and says, "I have a problem. . . . I have several options . . . what is your view?" Then he calls the next guy up and asks his opinion and, ultimately, comes up with the conclusion that, at best, will synthesize the group's thinking. A board contributes ideas— that's crucial.

While this director spoke for many, an equal number, while in favor of a sound relationship between the CEO and his board, felt the CEO's reliance on outside contact could be interpreted as a sign of inexperience. One told us:

> I think it's essential that the members of the board have a sound relationship among themselves and with the CEO. I don't mean that they all have to be the best of friends, but they should be able to get a decision made effectively, under the basic leadership or guidance of the CEO. I don't think you would want to have the CEO calling up all the time whenever he has any sort of problem or concern, because then the directors will get the feeling that he has no opinion and is relying too much on the board. Some CEOs will be in touch more often than others, but that is really a function of how much experience they've had as CEO and how confident they feel. The more experience the CEO has had, the less frequently he will call.

As we shall explain more fully in the next chapter, another reason for CEO-director contact is that many CEOs feel it is prudent to keep directors advised of important impending decisions before meetings. Thus, while the directors feel they are counseling the CEO, the latter feels he or she is keeping the directors informed and getting their ideas prior to a meeting. As we shall see, however, this seemingly positive behavior can also lead to further CEO control of the board. In any case, the boardroom, rather than outside interaction is where directors feel they make their major contributions.

Conclusions

Directors, like any group of individuals, view the same issues differently, agreeing more strongly on some than on others. They are less divided on issues of specific duties, such as ensuring legal and ethical conduct and selecting, advising, and evaluating the CEO, than they are on their impact on boardroom decisions.

Through the all-important CEO's report, they remain in

touch with the company's past performance and future plans, evaluating, at the same time, the CEO. Given the CEO's vital role in corporate success, such evaluation seems natural, but, given the CEO's power advantage, the emphasis on evaluation may strike some as an exercise in futility. The power imbalance may also explain why CEOs seem unconcerned about being judged by their directors, particularly when a CEO believes he's doing a good job.

Any real challenge or threat of replacement, as both directors and CEOs know, occurs only in extreme situations. In the past, many CEOs probably preferred to have directors assessing their performance rather than meddling in corporate strategy issues.

Some CEOs may still feel this way, but times are changing. Directors are becoming more involved in strategic issues. However, there are still important constraints on the exercise of their legal power.

In Chapter 3, we examined the constraint imposed by the board's lack of consensus about its accountability. In the next chapter, we take a detailed look at how time limitations and complexity of information constrain directors, keeping in mind that, despite real progress, corporate leaders—particularly the CEO—still have the power to subvert the board's ability to govern.

Chapter 5

The Balance of Power
in Normal Times

From the traditional legal perspective, directors control the affairs of the corporation through a legal mandate. In reality, executing their duties requires sufficient power to influence strategic direction, ensure legal and ethical conduct, and to choose, evaluate, and reward the CEO. Ultimately the board also needs the power to remove the CEO, but since this is a crisis situation, and our focus is still on its normal duties, we will deal with such crises in Chapters 6 and 7.

Because the term *power* can evoke images of a struggle between competing forces, we remind the reader that this is not the sense in which we use the term. What we shall describe is the directors' perception of superior CEO power, the reasons for the imbalance, and the consequences for governance. Rather than an overt struggle, we will reveal a subtle set of behaviors developed by CEOs and directors to adapt to the superior power of the governed.

Superior Power of the Governed

We asked directors to indicate how much influence they had in specific decisions. They told us their greatest influence was in selecting a CEO (see Table 5-1) and the second-greatest was when a change of ownership was at issue. Clearly, the latter is not a normal event in American companies, although it is occurring with increasing regularity. Similarly, while CEO successions are often orderly and undramatic transfers of power, the infrequency with which they occur removes them, too, from the sphere of directors' normal activities.

Nonetheless, since directors perceive work relating to present and future CEOs as their paramount function, in that sense we will call it normal. In the other spheres of influence listed, all part of the board's ordinary work, directors ranked their impact as two or less on a five-point scale. Our interpretation is that directors are reporting less influence than they should have in order to exercise their legal mandate.

This conclusion is supported by another set of data—how much influence the directors believe the CEO has on the majority of board issues (see Table 5-2). Ninety-four percent of the directors placed the CEO in the top two categories. Interpreted another way, the mean influence for the CEOs was 1.6 (with 1 meaning a great deal and 5 meaning none), while, other than in CEO selection, where directors rated themselves at 1.8, and changes in ownership (1.9), every other score was two or lower (see Table 5-1).

Granting that the CEO's real power normally exceeds that of the directors, we don't want to minimize the importance of the directors' legal authority, since it's the foundation upon which their other power sources rest. We must make clear, too, that we found no support for the concept of total power for directors. Rather, the goal was a suitable balance. One director stated:

Table 5-1
Directors' Influence

(Scale: 1 = A Great Deal 5 = No Influence)	
Selecting a CEO	1.81
Change in ownership	1.94
Evaluating new board members	2.02
Nominating board members	2.45
Approval of capital requirements	2.51
Corporate social responsibilities	2.54
Capital structure	2.61
Legal matters	3.20

Table 5-2
Power of the CEO on the Majority of Board Issues
Percentage of Directors Responding

(Scale: 1 = A Great Deal	5 = None)
1	44%
2	55%
3	5.6%
4	.4%
5	0.0%

Corporate governance isn't something you can do by the book. The best directors I know are those who come to a board with a broad background and can offer knowledge and expertise to a CEO, but who don't attempt to disturb the delicate balance between corporate directorships and management. Unfortunately, there is no formula for how to do just that.

Another director was more specific.

Directors don't run the company. Their job is to select the people who will run the company, and to ensure that those people are doing the best job possible. If they feel that management is not meeting expectations, then it's their job to remedy the situation. They should not, however, be running the place; and if the CEO is calling all the time, then it's a pretty strong sign that perhaps he's not the right guy for the job. On the other hand, if a director is throwing his weight around, then he obviously doesn't understand his job and should be replaced.

The directors interviewed had a variety of opinions as to how problematic the CEO's greater power was. One director was comfortable with complete CEO dominance.

The CEO shapes the board very much the way he wants, not only bringing people in, but also getting people he doesn't like off the board. He does this by relegating the obstinate director to a lesser committee, farther away from the executive committee. Other times, a CEO will simply say, "We've been friends a

*long time, but you're obviously not comfortable with
the management's policies and we need to have total
agreement here." Usually, the director will decide he's
not comfortable and get himself off the board.*

This director's view, that the CEO had sufficient power to
remove consistently dissenting directors, was an extreme one,
shared by few others.

Another director gave us this example of CEO dominance:

*Once, I got off a board when the CEO really wanted
to dominate the entire decision-making process. He was
going to make the decisions and was going to wave the
annual report in front of the shareholders and say,
"Look at what a supportive board I have." That's why I
got off. It cost me a lot of money, because I owned a lot
of stock that was going up for sale, but I didn't think he
was a good person. He basically didn't trust people,
and later events proved that I was right—he was neither a good person nor a good CEO.*

More typically, directors were concerned about the less
blatant ways in which CEOs could use their power. One director compared the styles of two CEOs.

*In the early days at [company name] [the first CEO]
tended to have sort of a heavy-handed style, and he
generally rammed things through the board. His successor has a much more consultative style. All of the CEOs
I know make it clear they're in charge. They have control over committee appointments, they can open or
shut issues, and they certainly control the agenda. . . .*

Another director spoke of an even subtler CEO influence.

*The CEO can influence his board, in my opinion,
through a variety of means: the agenda, his personality,
the forcefulness with which he puts forward proposals.
Of those, the last two are more influential. You know, it
does affect your role as a director. You don't go voting
down a CEO unless you have a hell of a good reason.
For one thing, it doesn't do the company any good. I'd
say, according to the rules of the game, you can ques-*

tion as hard as you want—and I've been on boards where you were really encouraged to ask aggressive, penetrating, even irritating questions—but unless these questions bring out something that is really flawed in the argument of the presentation, there's no way you're going to get the votes to have anything changed.

This director was suggesting that because the CEO controls the discussion process, he or she can ignore the toughest kinds of questions, if he or she wishes, since it's against boardroom norms for directors to object unless there's a clear defect around which the outside directors can rally.

Some directors were, at least on the surface, less concerned about the power imbalance because they thought fewer CEOs were misusing their power. One director, an active CEO himself, said:

I think every director is probably concerned about whether he or she thinks it's possible to contribute enough. The biggest inhibiting factor is the CEO. If he wants participation, he will arrange it so there is plenty of time for discussion. If he doesn't want participation, then there will be wonderful presentations to take up all the time. That is a pretty standard thing—you just see one presentation after another. I would say, however, that the age of the imperial CEO is vanishing.

Another director agreed. "The CEO has a large influence over whether he desires, or does not desire, his directors to function as true directors. He can do a variety of things to keep them quiet. It's clear today that CEOs, or at least most of them, are trying to do something smart with their directors."

While assertions such as "The age of the imperial CEO is vanishing," and "Most CEOs try to do something smart with their directors" seem clear and positive, they also recognize the potential for power abuse by CEOs, and suggest it still occurs. It's hard to know if these directors are wishing the problem away, or if they truly see it as less significant today.

In any event, most directors acknowledge that the CEO has greater power under normal conditions. From our data, however, we believe that imbalance has created two basic problems. First, a governance system cannot work if those who are supposed to govern lack the real power to do so. Even though most CEOs may not abuse their power, there is ample latitude for a devious, intransigent, or greedy CEO to do so. Recent examples—Harold Grey at United Technologies refusing to step down, or the leveraged buyout attempted by Russ Johnson at RJR-Nabisco—illustrate the abuse of CEO power. Such situations create crises in the boardroom, and even if the directors are ultimately able to resolve the crisis, the process is long and difficult, and can be damaging, sometimes fatal, to the corporation and its stockholders.

Second, because of its impact on discussions and decision making in the boardroom, the power imbalance can convert everyday problems into crises, when the directors' collective wisdom and judgment aren't brought forth in frank deliberations among themselves and with the CEO. We believe this is one reason why some boards have been slow, or unable, to deal with managerial and strategic problems facing their companies. In order to understand how and why this situation has developed, we need to examine the sources of a CEO's power and the limits on the directors' use of their legal authority.

The CEO's Power

Having earlier touched upon the main sources of CEO power, we want to look more closely at how directors view them.

Knowledge

The CEO's major power source, relative to directors', rests in a comprehensive knowledge of company affairs (see Table 5-3). In the boardroom, the CEO is the acknowledged expert. Outside directors are part-timers, while the CEO not only spends most of the time leading the company, he or she has usually been involved with it for his or her whole career.[1] Because of their experiences elsewhere, outside directors re-

---

1. Gordon Donaldson and Jay W. Lorsch, *Decision Making at the Top* (New York: Basic Books, 1982), p. 17.

Table 5-3
Sources of CEO's Power

(Scale: 1 = Very Important	5 = Not Important)
Knowledge of company affairs	1.22
Control of the meetings	2.07
Selection of agenda items	2.31
Selection of information for review	2.36
Selection of board members	2.56

spect the CEO's knowledge and experience. As one director put it:

> It's a difficult task, because outside directors often have no intimate knowledge of the specific business that will be discussed during the meeting. They are undoubtedly schooled and skilled in the principles of corporate business, but they probably lack intimate details of the current problems the company is facing. They have to rely on the CEO or the top management staff members to make propositions.

Knowledgeable, seasoned executives and professionals who are outside directors are keenly aware of the limitations of their own information and understanding, and readily concede that the CEO's grasp of company affairs is, by far, the most significant source of power.

One director summarized the respect so many have for their CEO's knowledge:

> I would say the CEO has a certain unique power over the board. He's the only guy who knows the operations of the firm in depth. He's an expert on the company and that fact alone puts constraints on directors. For example, they may know he came up in the mill and learned all the workings of the company from the bottom up. The directors, on the other hand, may have just joined the board and they may devote, at most, three days a month to the company.[2] They are coming from a different perspective and definitely feel a sense

---

2. According to available data, as we saw in Chapter 1, this estimate of time is extremely high for the typical director.

of inferiority to the CEO, and other inside directors, in terms of knowledge.

Control of the Board Meeting

Power also emanates from the CEO's control of the board meeting. The CEO creates the agenda, determines what information directors receive in advance, and, at the meetings, leads the discussions around the board table. Typical comments from directors include:

> *I think the CEO determines how effective a board is through the way he sets up the agenda, the way he arranges presentations, and the amount of discussion he schedules. There are lots of ways to avoid discussion if a CEO wants to. . . .*

> *I think the CEO influences the composition of the board first, and sets the tone of what's considered on the agenda, what information is available, how issues are dealt with in committee or by the full board, and who is put on which committee. The CEO can, and should, have a lot of influence on the way a board functions. But a good CEO will not dictate.*

Thus, one basic difficulty is that directors see most problems through the eyes of the CEO, who, like a multitalented filmmaker, writes the script, assigns the roles, directs the production, and has the starring role! While the growing importance of committees can reduce this problem, it cannot eliminate it, as one director explained.

> *The CEO sets the agenda—that is the key point. He makes available what he wants you to hear. Counter to that is a very strong committee structure, where the chairman of each committee decides what will be discussed and, to that extent, the committee exercises its own will and strength. . . . I would say that the feeling a director gets is a function of the presentation tone that the chairman uses. "Yes, we've got some problems, but they're not that bad and next month we're really going to turn things around." That CEO sets the tone and the board will go along with it . . . they don't know all*

*the details of the operation. How that chairman con-
ducts those meetings, whom he calls upon, who he has
making those reports can directly affect the board's perceptions—good or bad, up or down—it's all a function
of the chairman. Once again, though, committees can
ameliorate that.*

Better information and more probing by committees can
help, but basically, directors are swayed by the CEO's explanation of the situation and his or her decisions, and the manner
in which the CEO orchestrates boardroom events and discussions. As long as they trust the CEO, they are generally willing
to accept that interpretation of the company, its problems, and
those decisions and this is at the heart of the CEO's power in
the boardroom. But to understand the situation fully, we need
to look at the factors directors identify as constraints on their
contributions to boardroom discussions (see Table 5-4).

Constraints on Directors' Power

What these data first indicate is that almost half the directors report that they feel no constraints. No shrinking
violets, these successful and self-confident people, predomi-
nantly CEOs, are not easily intimidated or inhibited. Several
directors described themselves this way:

*I'm very outspoken. I don't know about other direc-
tors, but I never feel inhibited at all. In fact, I have al-*

Table 5-4
Constraints on Directors' Contribution (% Responding)*

Feel no constraints	49%
Little time at meeting	28%
Lack of expertise	22%
Lack of information	22%
Little time for preparation	17%
Dominance of CEO	16%
Not wanting to appear domineering	15%
Dominance of other outsiders	7%
Dominance of inside directors	3%

*Directors were asked to indicate which items, if any, constrained their
contributions. Thus, the total adds up to more than 100%.

ways felt whether I was the CEO or an outside director,
that the real value of a director is his knowledge; and if
directors don't level with their CEO, then they really
aren't needed.

No, I've never had that problem [feeling inhib-
ited]—I've never hesitated to say what I thought at this
company or any other firm where I've been a director.
Nor have I felt that there has been any pressure of
"don't rock the boat," "peace at any price," "let the
game go on as it is."

If the management doesn't let me say my piece,
then I don't stick around. I've never actually had that
problem, but I wouldn't stick around long if I had. . . .

The other half, however, don't share that unfettered view
and do feel constrained in their ability to contribute. This
response, combined with the Chapter 4 data that about one-
third of the directors feel they contribute only moderately at
board meetings, further indicates the potential for improving
the governance process. Those who felt constrained, however,
ranked the dominance of the CEO as relatively unimportant.
In fact, 83% of all directors indicated the CEO's dominance
wasn't a constraint, despite acknowledging his or her superior
power.[3]

One explanation of the seeming paradox is board members' assertiveness and self-confidence. Another is the way
most CEOs lead boardroom discussions. As we shall amplify
shortly, they seem to encourage discussion and contribution
from directors, and directors report feeling less inhibited by
the CEO than by their own lack of time (28%), expertise (22%),
and information (22%). However, their belief in freedom from
CEO dominance is often an illusion, but one that is part of a
clear pattern that limits the impact many directors actually
have in discussions with knowledgeable CEOs and other top
managers.

Information, Expertise, and Time

Seasoned directors recognize the complexity of the issues
before them and, cognizant of their own lack of in-depth

3. Forty-nine percent feel no constraint and 34% feel constrained, but not by the
   CEO.

knowledge, they are reluctant to speak up. Several directors explained:

> Yes, there have been times when I felt my ability to contribute has been inhibited, but those tend to be times when the nature of the subject matter encourages me to bow to experience and knowledge. In those situations, I tend to suppress my own instinctive position, in the face of a contrary position taken by a respected peer. I am not the type to be inhibited in any other way.

> I've never felt inhibited by the actions of others, but I think one would be foolish to think he or she was equally versed on every subject. There are some subjects that you can ask obvious questions about, and there would be some subjects on which you would be unable to ask in-depth questions, because you wouldn't understand the answers.

> I feel I contribute less than most of the other directors because I'm a lawyer, not a businessman. Consequently, I say more on the less routine things, such as mergers, the technical aspects, the legal aspects, and the so-called fit aspects of the firm, which decide whether or not a proposal fits in with the nature of the existing firm.

Such comments underline how much these people respect knowledge and experience; and how their respect for expertise and their natural desire not to appear foolish in front of peers inhibit them. The importance of protecting one's own self-esteem was addressed by one director who referred to the disappearing breed of directors who have "inherited their seats":

> I sit on a few boards today where we have a few guys who sit like bumps on a log, and when they walk away, I know they are embarrassed. But they'll be off in a few years, and the level of discussion is just too far ahead of them most of the time. They're afraid to ask a dumb question because they've done that a few times and they're embarrassed as a result of it. But there is a fair amount of peer pressure . . . you don't go unpre-

*pared to a board meeting. You ought to be prepared to
enter into any discussion, particularly the hot issues.*

However, it isn't only the "bumps on the log" who don't want
to be embarrassed. Other directors, too, will remain silent to
save face.

The lack of adequate preparation time constrains 17% of
the directors, and explains the apparent contradiction between the Chapter 4 data that directors receive all the necessary information, and this chapter's data, which contend that
lack of information inhibits their contribution. The latter data
imply that, without enough time to digest all the information,
and without specific expertise in certain business lines, directors aren't always equipped to understand the underlying assumptions of management's proposals. This lack, of course,
increases their dependence on management, particularly on
the CEO. As one director said:

> *One problem a board will often have is making
> sure that management is able to concisely present the
> facts and the issues, and not just give you a stack of pa-
> pers, a mile high, to sift through. A board has to de-
> pend upon management to provide information in a
> way the director can get his hands around. You know
> this isn't a 2,000-hour-a-year job, so you have to have
> some organization and brevity. Some managements are
> better at it than others—the good ones know how to
> highlight the pertinent themes.*

A second director emphasized this point. "A good CEO
will know what kind of information, and how much, to send.
If he sends way too much, it will only serve to prolong the
meeting, which doesn't do anyone any good."

An active CEO raised the question of balance.

> *I think there's a uniform desire on the part of the
> operating management to provide sufficient informa-
> tion. The question is how much is too much, and how
> much distillation and organization around a point of
> view should be undertaken? It's either "Here are the
> books—tell me what you think," or should they lay out*

the issues and do a lot of work around some of them? There's a continuing process of working through how much, and in what shape, is enough. Most of the time, some people on the board feel they don't get enough, while others feel they're getting too much to deal with. There will never be a perfect amount.

However, beyond the constraints already addressed in this chapter, directors considered the issue of time to discuss and digest information *at the actual board meeting* to be their major constraint (28%).

With the typical board meeting lasting 3 to 6 hours, at 5 to 9 meetings a year, time to address—and assess—complex data and issues is necessarily limited.[4] Much of a typical meeting, as we discussed in Chapter 4, is devoted to the CEO's report, financial performance review, and routine legal matters. As we've also noted, CEOs can, whether by chance or design, schedule so many management presentations that discussion time may be as elusive as the Loch Ness monster. Finally, for some directors, the discussion time is affected by the size of the board itself. As one director explained:

I feel more comfortable speaking during a committee meeting, because we have more time and we're more relaxed. Furthermore, as a group of 5 or 6 people, rather than a full board of 15 or 16, it's easier to communicate ideas and get things done. As a result, we probably talk about things that we wouldn't discuss at the full board meetings.

Another director made a similar point. "I suppose there is a relationship between the board's performance and the CEO's personality, but I think it's almost more a function of the board's size. I'm on one board with over 30 members. When a board is very, very big, half of the directors aren't going to say anything."

While such a large board is unusual in industrial companies, obviously the more people in the room, the harder it is

4. Heidrick & Struggles, *The Changing Board* (1987), p. 4. Fifty-five and three tenths percent of the *Fortune* 100 companies met 5 to 9 times a year and 34.1% met 10 to 14 times a year.

for each to get time to speak. One director, however, felt the problem lay less with the clock than with some of his colleagues.

> We are encouraged to participate, and we're given more than enough time to share our opinions . . . the only limitations, in my personal opinion, are the effusive talkers who go on and on, and bore me—and, at times, my own lack of knowledge about a particular subject. . . .

Fortunately, domineering directors are a minority. Only 15% of our directors felt themselves constrained through a fear of being seen as overbearing; only 7% considered that the dominance of outside directors constrained other board members; and a scant 3% complained of inside-director dominance. Directors, we concluded, are generally considerate of one another. Such consideration, however, given the time pressures of a meeting, may further limit their ability to contribute as fully as they might wish.

Protecting One's Image

No one likes to look foolish and directors are no exception, as a final piece of data illustrates. While 51% of directors felt completely free to voice minority opposition, of the 49% who occasionally felt inhibited in taking a minority stand, it was uncertainty about the correctness of their own position that constrained them. Directors can be as unwilling as an unprepared child in a classroom quiz to raise their hands and venture a wrong answer.

Again, we see how directors value knowledge, information, and expertise—their own or that of others. When they believe the CEO's knowledge surpasses theirs, they often retreat from a minority dissent, but when they believe their understanding equals the CEO's, they usually feel free to stand in opposition.

For the half who never feel inhibited in voicing minority opinions, we can only speculate that they are generally better informed or, more likely, that they serve on boards where such freedom is actively encouraged. A small number of boards, we suppose, may have some effusive talkers who "go on and on," whether knowledgeable or not!

For most directors, however, the CEO's power is appropriately rooted in the capability to fully inform and advise them about the company. As directors *do*, however, have thoughts on how CEOs can best interact with them, we will examine their preferences, as well as the ways in which CEOs build relationships with their boards.

CEO Style

How CEOs deal with outside directors is a major determinant of how well the governance process works in specific companies. Directors are as clear on this as they are that CEOs have different ways of dealing with the board. Several directors explained.

> *The character of the CEO determines how he'll relate to the board. You'll find those who would much prefer to have a board meeting once a year, because the only reason they have a board meeting is that the shareholders and legislators say you should have one. It really depends on the individual, but I think the best CEOs are those who communicate openly and frequently with outside directors.*

> *Some people like to run a one-man band and the board is there to say, "We agree"; other people use their boards better on the basis of seeking out their input.*

> *CEOs are as varied as humans are. There is no stereotype. They range from reticent to outgoing. You can't put a CEO in a book. The more outgoing he is, the better his relationship with the board. . . . A successful CEO has to develop a rapport with the board. The ones that don't are in jeopardy.*

As we explained earlier, some directors are concerned about CEOs at the domineering end of the spectrum. Further, the natural bias of CEOs may cause some to inadvertently—or deliberately—shape agendas and select data in ways that in-

fluence board decisions. Even if such abuses occasionally occur, we believe the greater danger to effective governance is
more subtle. Because of directors' dependence on and respect
for the CEO, many boards have developed a delicate way of
dealing with the CEO. In turn, what directors describe as
"good CEOs" deal equally carefully with directors. We can
better understand the relationship by describing what directors consider the best style for a CEO. The following comments
are typical.

> The best CEO is relatively open with his board, and
> seeks their advice and counsel when pertinent issues
> present themselves. So yes, I do think that there is a
> correlation between the personality of the CEO—or
> should I say the style that he uses in running the board
> meetings—and the overall effectiveness of those meet-
> ings.

> If the CEO is introverted and doesn't welcome dis-
> cussion, then the board will be almost useless. The
> wider, and more open, the discussion, the better the de-
> cisions the board will make.

> If you have an autocratic CEO, then he won't draw
> out the input from the various directors. He'll deliver
> his speech at each meeting, and it will be a monologue.
> If you have a person who is more sensitive to the per-
> sonalities of the directors, and to human nature as well,
> then he'll direct the discussions and put his views on
> the table—but he will invite discussion and participa-
> tion from the board. So the personality of the CEO has
> a lot to do with the quality of discussion that you have
> and, by and large, I think CEOs prefer to have an open
> discussion.

Directors want a CEO who facilitates discussion without
dominating or slanting it, who is open, who frequently encourages them to express their views, and who seeks their
counsel. Most fundamentally, they want one who develops a
rapport with them and demonstrates trust in them. Such a CEO
doesn't flaunt power but invites the directors to help lead the

company. While the board recognizes the CEO's control over board-meeting content and process, and influence in selecting new directors, it, nonetheless, wants to share that power.

Leading a board in this manner poses a challenge, as one U.K. CEO, also director of an American company, explained:

> I feel that the way I manage the nonexecutive directors is a true test of my leadership abilities. If I feel I cannot get them to work together effectively, then I'm not doing my job effectively. There are many situations when a CEO would prefer to say to his directors, "To hell with all of you! Resign if you don't like what I'm doing!" than to patiently work through the problem himself. He doesn't do this, though, because if he did, he wouldn't have a board left.

A retired CEO agreed. "A CEO has to be smart enough not to be too domineering, so that he can get the best out of his directors."

Norms in the Boardroom

All of this sounds positive—and obvious. A CEO who is open with directors, who seeks their advice and counsel, who encourages discussion, will naturally get more from the directors than a CEO who does none of these things.

As one CEO-director said: "There's no sense in having a board if the directors don't feel able to say what they think. Candor and realism are essential, as well as having a CEO who will put the problems on the table, in front of the board, and address issues with aggressive honesty."

However, despite an appearance of openness and candor, the reality is often different. A subtle set of unspoken norms, in fact, dictates the actual course of behavior in the boardroom. Even the ideal outward behavior of a CEO doesn't necessarily result in effective contributions from directors.

For example, an effective CEO is expected to keep his directors informed of important issues and events between meetings—and to solicit their views.

One director said:

> The most effective CEOs are those who keep their
> board members well informed, and structure decisions
> carefully through the directors. You can't do that just
> with the board meeting—you have to do it outside the
> meeting. Maybe you'll use a committee, for instance.

A second director elaborated:

> The CEO who goes to a board meeting and doesn't,
> at least generally, know how each of the individual di-
> rectors feels about the issues to be discussed, has not
> done his work. In the first place, he hasn't gotten the
> directors' input; in the second place, he hasn't given
> them his input. Now, he may know they're not all in
> accord with him, but at least he would know
> everybody's views, because in the final analysis, he's
> really the judge—he has to make a decision.

Again, this sounds positive, but, rather than encouraging
open disagreement in actual board meetings, preliminary discussions can reduce the healthy give-and-take of conflict, because so many issues may have been privately decided by the
CEO before the meeting.

A second U.K. CEO, who also served on a U.S. board,
explained the extrameeting contact this way:

> In the United States, the CEO will often contact di-
> rectors individually, when an issue arises, rather than
> discuss it with the entire group. I think the rationale be-
> hind this is that (a) it's a waste of time to use every-
> body and (b) it's the fear of losing control. If you get the
> whole group of outside directors, who outnumber you
> 10 to 1, together, it is quite a concern. This isn't the
> case in the U.K., mainly because we have a more bal-
> anced ratio, and many of the nonexecutive directors are
> well aware of what the management has in mind for the
> future. The way I see it: What could conceivably be
> wrong with having all the issues out on the table in the
> open for people to contribute upon?

Our interviews did not reveal why the CEOs who sought prior contact with directors did so. We suspect, however, that this British visitor to a U.S. boardroom has hit the nail on the head.

The informal rules for directors are also well defined. Directors are expected, above all, to treat the CEO with respect, which means not embarrassing him or her in a board meeting. This understanding may also explain why directors welcome between-meeting exchanges with the CEO, as they are expected to deal discreetly, wherever possible, with any disagreement about the CEO's position on an issue. As one director explained: "I'll tell you, if you have a serious objection to what the CEO is saying, and you get the agenda in advance, you shouldn't surprise the CEO and blast him out of the water." His attitude is understandable, if we recall directors' own sensitivity to appearing ill informed.

Since directors shouldn't openly criticize the CEO, or the CEO's positions, the accepted way of objecting is to ask penetrating questions. If other directors join in and the tone of the discussion becomes increasingly critical, the message sent is one of disapproval. Under normal circumstances, such disapproval is rarely made explicit in a board meeting.

There are also norms about how to deal with fellow directors, one of which is not to assert leadership over them. All are peers on the board, and being openly assertive is bad form. As we discussed earlier, this norm also implies not hogging discussion time.

Also de rigueur is not contacting fellow directors outside of meetings. One director explained:

> That's taboo. We feel that would be dealing behind the chairman's back. Of course, there are conversations on outings or buses. You make an observation about the capability of someone and discuss it casually. But we never have a so-called rump meeting, where we would discuss things with the chairman not present. We feel we have a relationship with the chairman, that we can say anything to the chairman, and that's the only way to do it. There's no point dealing cards behind anyone's back.

A final norm in most boards, as we explained in Chapter 3, is for directors to refer exclusively to their responsibility to shareholders, rather than to other constituencies or to the corporation itself. As we indicated, directors don't explicitly discuss their accountabilities at all. In fact, in many boardroom discussions, the outcome of all these norms is "undiscussability!"[5]

The core matters on directors' minds remain unarticulated in meetings, leaving CEOs, and other directors, obliged to read very subtle cues. The kinds of questions raised might be oblique references to earlier private conversations with the CEO, or "advice" offered to the CEO in the guise of "ideas," oblique hints designed to send a stronger message.

Why so many boards develop such norms is not entirely clear from our data, but the norms have existed for many years.[6] We believe one reason they've developed, and that they persist, is the power reversal between the CEO and the board. One way to handle an ambiguous and complicated social relationship is to avoid discussing it. Certainly, a situation in which directors are supposed to govern a more powerful CEO, who, in most cases, is also chairman of the board, is rife with ambiguity and complexity.

Sensitive CEOs alleviate this problem by keeping directors informed, by seeking their advice between meetings, and by conducting open and frank discussions. But the discussions aren't as open and frank as the words normally imply. In return for the CEO's considerate behavior, directors who are sensitive about their images also want to protect the CEO's image, and do so by behaving within the norms.

While this attitude sounds reasonable, it produces meetings that often resemble a charade of productive, problem-

5. Chris Argyris, *Strategy Change and Defensive Routines* (Boston: Pitman, 1985), p. 76.
6. Myles Mace, *Directors: Myth and Reality* (Boston: Division of Research, Harvard Business School, 1971), and Thomas J. Whisler, "Rules of the Game: Inside the Board Room," selected papers, University of Chicago Graduate School of Business, October 1987, based on a book of the same name published by Dow Jones–Irwin in 1984.

solving discussions. The directors-CEOs would be concerned if management meetings in their own companies were characterized by such norms. Similarly, social psychologists and management experts would dub these meetings as very poor decision-making forums. The purpose of a group discussion of an issue is to discuss diverse points of view openly, and to confront and resolve differences of opinions.[7] Boards that follow the norms we've described don't meet this standard.

As a result, our evidence indicates that in many boardrooms important issues aren't discussed openly, nor in a timely fashion. These issues may include the declining performance of the company's core business, and whether the decline is temporary or cyclical or an indication of a more serious long-term deterioration; or the impact of a decision on the short- and long-term value of the company's stock. The biggest taboo, however, is against open criticism of the CEO's activities—about how he or she is shaping the agenda, conducting the meetings, or, on a broader level, adequately developing a successor or being forceful enough in correcting performance problems in a faltering division.

With so many topics publicly undiscussable, boards often react too slowly when issues arise and allow small, manageable problems to fester and grow into major crises. We believe this tendency has contributed to the current problems experienced by some U.S. companies.

In part, this happens because few boards are highly cohesive groups. Directors normally get together only at board meetings, where time for informal give-and-take is limited. In addition, the boardroom norms we've described tend to discourage clear and meaningful discussions, without which directors are unlikely to form a tightly knit group. This is unfortunate, because as directors often reminded us, their numbers constitute an important source of their power to govern. When the 8 or 10 outside directors on a board agree on an issue, it is difficult for any but the most intransigent CEO to resist.

7. See, for example, Paul R. Lawrence and Jay W. Lorsch, *Organization and Environment* (Boston: Division of Research, Harvard Business School, 1967).

Conclusions

"United we stand; divided we fall" might be an apt motto for America's directors. Though they are legally empowered to govern, in reality, the CEO controls most of the power levers in the boardroom.

While few CEOs abuse their power, the norms of polite boardroom behavior discourage directors from openly questioning or challenging the CEO's performance or proposals, under normal conditions. Despite the fact that CEOs are expected to encourage director discussion and involvement, the reality falls far short of the ideal because of boardroom norms of conduct to which both CEOs and directors adhere.

When directors lack a forum, inside or outside the boardroom, to discuss tough issues together, to challenge management collectively, and to act quickly in crises, their numerical advantage over the CEO cannot easily translate into real strength.

The reluctance to violate group norms and the practical obstacles to unity may not create problems in healthy companies, but, as we will illustrate in subsequent chapters, they can delay the recognition of emerging problems and create serious difficulties for boards dealing with crises, as so many do in modern corporate America.

Chapter 6

Crisis Management
in the Boardroom

"Directors are like firemen. They sit around doing
very little until there's a fire alarm and then they spring
into action."

While this director's description underestimates the
board's normal importance, it illustrates the belief of many that
directors play their most significant role during a crisis. The crises
to which they refer are typical of those that have dotted the
business landscape in recent years: possible changes in ownership—whether by friendly or unfriendly takeovers or leveraged buyouts; the unexpected death or incapacity of the
CEO; an unanticipated environmental crisis such as Bhopal;
legal action against the company; serious dissension among
top managers; the CEO's failure to perform his or her job; and,
of course, sustained declines in the performance of the company and/or the entire industry.

This may suggest that each kind of crisis has a unique
effect on directors' ability to govern. In fact, the evidence presented here and in the next chapter, drawn mainly from four
case studies, identifies two sets of variables that can help directors anticipate the problems they will confront. Understanding the pattern should also help those concerned with
improving corporate governance to identify the changes that
will allow directors to be more effective both in crises and in
normal times. One set of forces affecting directors' real power

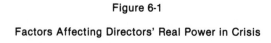

Figure 6-1

Factors Affecting Directors' Real Power in Crisis

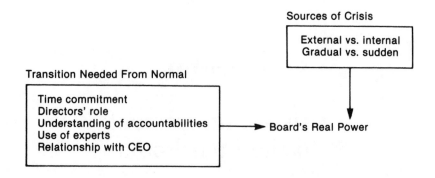

is when, and from where, the crisis emanates. The second is the extent to which the crisis forces the board to change its normal mode of operations, including its relationship with the CEO (see Figure 6-1).

Sources of Crisis

The difficulty directors have in governing in a crisis depends on whether it comes primarily from within the firm or from outside, and whether it occurs suddenly and is clear to all involved or whether it has evolved gradually and its significance is only slowly understood. For example, an unfriendly takeover attempt or friendly acquisition offer comes from outside the firm and is clear and sudden. Directors have no difficulty recognizing either problem or understanding its causes. They also realize that their actions will be scrutinized by the business press and the financial community and are likely to lead to legal actions, which, because of the business judgment doctrine, necessitate the advice of legal and investment banking experts.

While the death or incapacity of a CEO is an equally sudden and clear event, it is an internal one. If directors and managers have performed their normal job of assuring competent succession, it may be a short-lived event with little, if any, external notice.

Gradual crises emerge slowly. The decline of an entire industry, such as the American steel industry, or the rise of new competitors, such as the Japanese consumer electronic companies, are examples of gradual, primarily externally caused, crises. Often, those involved understand the magnitude of such trends only in hindsight. An internal example is the failing performance of the CEO, whose inadequacy becomes apparent when company performance falters, something that may not happen for years. While directors may gradually sense dissension among subordinate managers, this realization usually develops over time, since loyalty to the CEO is a strong norm among managers and directors.

While company performance can decline because of a cataclysmic event, the more typical examples occur as a combination of long-term industry decline, competitor actions, and the failure of internal management. Therefore, we have categorized such problems as gradual, yet both external and internal in nature (see Figure 6-2).

A final set of data from our questionnaire suggests why the source of the crisis is important to our understanding of directors' problems; we asked directors how they would re-

Figure 6-2

Sources of Crisis

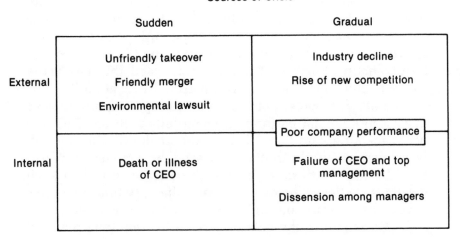

Table 6-1
Responses to a Persistent Financial Performance Shortfall

(Scale: Always = 1, Sometimes = 2, Never = 3)

Evidence	Confront CEO at Board Meeting	Contact Other Directors Privately
Financial performance data	1.24	1.60
Problem with debt service or covenants	1.33	1.74
Difficulty in refinancing	1.37	1.83
Internal management dissension	1.53	1.56
Organized investor initiatives	1.54	1.80
Adverse proxy returns	1.69	2.04
Unfavorable press coverage	1.83	2.16
Depressed market value of share	1.98	2.21

spond to "a persistent financial performance shortfall," depending upon the evidence available to them (see Table 6-1). They indicated they would be slightly more willing to break the norm against embarrassing the CEO in a meeting than they would be to violate the norm prohibiting private contact among directors. With one exception, the importance of the evidence that would stimulate either action was similar. The major trigger was clear evidence of financial difficulty, while the least important was the depressed price of the company's shares. As we suggested in Chapter 3, directors are skeptical about such signals from the stock market.

The exception to the consensus was that directors are most likely to contact each other privately when they become aware of management dissension. Apparently, they feel such a situation would be too embarrassing to the CEO to raise at a board meeting. Further, of all the factors listed, this may be the clearest indication that the CEO, personally, is at fault.

Eighty-one percent of the directors report that they have discussed financial performance shortfalls with the CEO in a board meeting, and 25% of those report the results were always positive, while another 55% say they were usually positive. Thus, two-thirds of all the directors involved in such meetings believe they've had an effect, while one-third haven't had discussions or believe they had little or no effect.

At first glance the data may seem to contradict much of

the evidence presented in earlier chapters. However, the questions were phrased in the context of "a persistent financial shortfall," which means several years of financial performance difficulties. Further, the evidence given in the questions all indicated a clear crisis, which suggests, as do the cases that follow, that when directors recognize a crisis, they will act. The difficulty, however, is that many crises are gradual—simmering and fermenting for years before their seriousness is recognized. During this period, the board too often conducts its affairs by the normal rules of conduct, which means not raising their concerns in a board meeting, or with one another privately.

In addition, none of our questions implied a CEO clearly at fault. However, when we asked directors what they would do "when you think the CEO is faltering in his or her duties and there is no evidence the situation would be remedied," the answer was very different, unequivocal, and consistent with the earlier data. Eighty-five percent of the directors indicated that the only way to deal with such a situation was to work for a consensus among the directors about the need for change, which is consistent with how they would deal with management dissension. When the crisis is internal and the CEO is part of the problem, directors facing the difficulty of gathering the power to act, arm their ultimate weapon—their power as a group.

Acting together has several benefits beyond the power it provides. First, it enables directors to be sure that their leader is in difficulty. In the complex world of large corporations, establishing that the CEO is at fault isn't an easy task. Second, it's emotionally grueling to dethrone the king. In most companies, the CEO has been the leader not only of the corporation but, more intimately from the directors' perspective, of the board itself, which makes challenging him even more painful. Moreover, many directors are present or past CEOs, with an understandable sympathy for a colleague. The support of other directors makes it easier to deal with a difficult and distasteful task.

But the central point, which is illustrated by the cases that follow, is that the most difficult crises directors face are those that are gradual and involve the CEO. In addition to contend-

ing with the CEO's superior power, directors must find ways
to agree that a long-smoldering series of brushfires is, in fact, a
major conflagration. Such agreement is key to mobilizing their
collective power.

From Normalcy to Crisis

The second set of forces affecting the difficulties directors
confront in a crisis is how much normal procedures must
change. The most obvious change is the need for a dramatic
increase in time commitment. Accounts of many long, special
board meetings accompanied descriptions of crises directors
had faced. Furthermore, the nature of directors' relationships
with the CEO and other managers may shift. In normal times,
as advisers to management, they ask penetrating questions,
rather than taking the lead, but, in many crises, they become
more obvious decision makers. A director described the
changes:

> If a company is running along smoothly, then it's
> advice and counsel that directors are called upon to
> give, but if there is some sort of crisis, then a director
> will have to devote far more time to study all of the
> ramifications of the issue in order to be able to make
> the right decision. In the case of a takeover, you have to
> meet constantly in order to fulfill your fiduciary respon-
> sibilities, or else you may be liable at some future date.

A second director made a similar point as he described a
specific internal crisis he had encountered.

> One [crisis] occurred when we lost a CEO unexpect-
> edly. Although there had been some succession plan-
> ning, it was not well developed because he had recently
> been brought in from the outside, and there wasn't a
> great deal of pressure to worry about who would be
> next in line. We had just been through that whole mess.
> Anyway, the executive committee met day after day,
> considering new candidates for the position right in the
> midst of the corporation's strategic responsibilities. . . .
> This is a time when the relationship between manage-

*ment and the board is critical, because the board is act-
ing out its principal role [ensuring a smooth transition
of leadership], but it has to do so with the best interests of the top management and the entire company in
mind.*

While this director was comfortable with the need to take
account of top management and the future of the company,
many other directors said that another change, in many crises,
was a heightened tension between their narrow responsibility
to shareholders and their broader concerns for the survival of
the corporation and the well-being of other constituencies.
One director described an unfriendly takeover offer.

*It [a takeover] happens at such a fast pace that a
director can do no more than just keep his eyes focused
on his primary obligation and that is "What the hell is
in the best interest of the shareholders and how do you
protect them?" And from that, then what about the
other stakeholders in this enterprise and what consequences flow to them—including employees, customers,
communities, and the general sense of what's right for
this country? But the primary issue has to be, because
that's our legal obligation, how do you protect the
shareholders' interests longer term and short term? At
some level of offer and at some level of complication,
the scale tips and you can no longer persuade yourself
that to resist a takeover attempt is in the best interest of
the shareholder. Even though you know that there are
likely to be other consequences of that move which you
wouldn't particularly welcome, the numbers have just
reached a level where you become persuaded that no
matter what you think the long-term prospects of the
enterprise are, and what benefits would flow to the
shareholder over the long term if you kept the company intact, the number being offered is sufficiently
high that you'd have to say "yes" at that level. You'd
have to accept the offer.*

The tension directors feel about their accountabilities creates problems not just for individuals, but for the board as a

group. Since board members are unlikely to have a common view of their accountabilities, or to be comfortable with an explicit discussion of it, the tension isn't easily resolved, making it hard for a board to develop the necessary sense of shared purpose, which will allow it to use its power as a group.

Directors' concern about accountabilities can't be separated from an awareness of possible legal entanglements. As we saw in Chapter 2, legal problems may not be a big worry, but directors would prefer to avoid them. The safest way to do so, under the business judgment doctrine, is to rely on outside experts for advice. This need brings lawyers and investment bankers into the boardroom more frequently than in normal times. One director described a typical experience:

> I was intimately involved in the whole situation at [company name], which was not a pleasant experience although it was very educational. In such a crisis, the directors are truly the sacrificial victims. They're harangued by lawyers as to the risks they will incur if they don't follow the lawyers' advice explicitly. Then, no matter what they do, they will be confronted with a lawsuit from one party or another. In these situations, you can't please everybody, and those who don't come out on the winning side feel that it's their right to get revenge—usually on the board members.

While many directors agree they become sacrificial lambs whose influence is eroded by outside experts, many others felt they didn't have to be so dependent upon outside advice. Another director represented this viewpoint.

> Board members should not allow the outside consultants to make their decisions for them in a crisis situation. They have to rely on the outside advisers to provide an assessment of the bid and of the future, but ultimately, it is up to the board to decide. I think that the reaction to the outside experts is changing. I'm on the [company name] board and, when we initially made a bid for [other company name], I really didn't agree with the packaging of the price. The experts had so many fancy overheads with graphs and figures that it was hard to disagree. Today, however, I wouldn't

> *hesitate to challenge any figure an investment banker
> flashed in front of me.*

Regardless of how directors feel about legal and financial experts during a crisis, the experts' boardroom presence complicates the directors' task of gaining control.

How much crises can alter the relationship between the directors and the CEO depends upon the nature of the crisis. At one extreme is a sudden external threat, such as an unfriendly takeover situation, where the CEO and the board stand united against a common enemy. In this situation there is little change. As one director described it:

> *The CEO's responsibility throughout the whole
> crisis is to marshal the forces together and to locate experts
> like investment bankers and top law firms to provide
> the best possible advice available. It's up to the
> outside directors, in this litigious society in which we
> live, to work to protect themselves, but they can do this
> by doing their homework and not second-guessing
> either the stockholders, whom they are there to represent,
> or any of the other parties involved. It is up to the
> directors to interact with the management to ensure
> that they are fulfilling their fiduciary responsibilities,
> but it's up to the CEO to define a logical course of action
> for them to follow.*

In such cases, the board accepts the CEO's leadership, understanding that it must also fulfill its responsibilities. However, when the CEO's performance or incapacity is at issue as the data above revealed, things get stickier because the board can no longer accept the CEO's leadership. A director described such a situation.

> *These things don't happen all that often because,
> from a practical point of view, it takes two to three
> years to realize it's the CEO who's lagging and then,
> usually, he will be nearing retirement age so it just
> won't be worth making a big stink about him. There are
> also ways to encourage a CEO to step down gracefully. I
> really think that a board needs some central figure to
> whom everyone can look when issues like this arise.*

With the CEO no longer their leader, the directors must find someone among their own number to act. Since the chairman and the CEO are generally the same person, one director must step forward and assume a leadership position. A director described his own emergence as a leader.

> I was recently involved in a major crisis at the bank. The whole bank got way out of hand in terms of its financial performance, and there were grumbles from both inside and outside directors that got louder and louder as the situation got worse. I organized the committee of outside directors that had an independent audit done. After what seemed like an endless stream of meetings, we voted to have the CEO removed and we ultimately brought in a new guy from another bank to take over.

But who will step forward to lead the board isn't clear-cut. A second director described how his personality and background thrust him to the fore.

> I would hope that I came to the realization of what was going on faster, because of the nature of my business. I really think though that they looked at me as the "businessman." Second, there was the fact that I wasn't scared of Joe [the CEO]. I'm a very blunt sort of fellow and I would speak out on everything at board meetings. I would just say, "Joe, I don't understand that." I still didn't after he explained it. I guess I led the fight because I had to—I had a moral responsibility to do so. It was more than a legal responsibility, which is what the shareholders hold you to; it was a personal thing. I couldn't have slept soundly for the rest of my life, not only because it was a question of legality, but because it was also one of morality. The first instinct was to suck your thumb, put your head on the pillow and cry, and just resign, but you can't do that. You have a stewardship for those shareholders, which was a rule when they had the first corporate director, and the rule is still true today. Of course, it would have been easier to resign, but I had a moral obligation. There is no compromise on that.

While some directors prefer passivity, crises involving the CEO require that people like these two men assert themselves. When one or more directors assume the mantle of leadership in a crisis, the CEO has to forfeit some power. One director agreed:

> Yes, I was involved in one situation that was particularly touchy for about a year. It involved a self-serving CEO who wanted to stay on beyond the normal retirement age. It was particularly difficult because factions began to develop among the board members, with the split separating those who had been long-term friends of the CEO, and those who had been brought on relatively recently for their particular expertise in some area. This particular half of the board already had another individual in mind for the CEO's position, and he had been primed for about four years to take over. Basically it was a fight similar to what took place at United Technologies, in a sense. It was very unpleasant because no one wanted to insult anyone else, but it was almost unavoidable.
>
> Well, there was a lot of complex maneuvering and I found myself in the middle of it since I had known the CEO for a long time, but I felt that it was important that he step down when his time came. What ultimately happened is that two of us sat down with the CEO and told him our view of the situation and agreed to let him remain on the board as a sort of associate chairman for one year before he really had to step out. It worked out very well.

Tipping the balance of power in the board's favor often requires the emergence of at least one outsider as a leader, but these informal leaders must be accepted by the majority of the other outside directors. This is often a delicate problem, since the assertiveness of one director, or even a small group of directors, violates normal ground rules and might lead to friction among directors, further complicating the need to build a consensus. When, as sometimes happens, the solution is a face-saving compromise—allowing the CEO to stay on until retirement or serve as vice chairman—we believe that, however humane a decision, it may prolong and complicate the

Figure 6-3

Case Studies[a]

	Sudden	Gradual
External	Martin Marietta Unfriendly takeover bid	Burlington Northern Industry decline Poor company performance
Internal	Dunntech Death of CEO	Harvest Dissension among management

[a] Although we have classified these case studies in the quadrant to which they primarily belong, subsequent events, in some instances, led to other forces also shaping the crisis.

resolution of the crisis. Thus, any situation where the board must gain the power to challenge an unwilling CEO is the most severe crisis directors can encounter.

Four Boards in Crises

Having identified the forces that shape the difficulty directors face in handling crises, we next turn to four cases that describe in more detail how directors dealt with those forces and how effectively they governed. The four cases represent the different sources of crises (see Figure 6-3). In the balance of this chapter, we shall examine the two situations in which there were sudden crises—at Martin Marietta and Dunntech.* In Chapter 7 we shall discuss the events at Burlington Northern and Harvest,* which were more gradual.

* Dunntech and Harvest are disguised names of actual companies. Other facts and numbers have also been changed to protect their identities and those of their directors and managers. However, the problems confronting the directors, and the ways in which they dealt with them, have been accurately portrayed. These disguises were necessary in order to use the cases. That both were internally generated crises we believe is further confirmation of the sensitive nature of such situations.

Martin Marietta: The Bendix Takeover

The Events

In April 1982, Tom Pownall was appointed chief executive officer of Martin Marietta Corporation, a Bethesda, Maryland–based producer of advanced aerospace products, aluminum, and cement. Four months later, he was entangled in one of the most widely publicized takeover battles in American corporate history, even though his predecessor, Don Rauth, still retained the title of chairman.

On August 25, Bendix Corporation, a diversified manufacturer of automotive components and production machinery, announced a cash tender offer for up to 45% of Martin Marietta's common shares at $43 a share. Bendix reported that it already owned roughly 4.5% of Martin Marietta's outstanding common shares, and that it intended to follow the initial offer with a proposal to exchange Bendix shares for the remaining Martin Marietta shares at a ratio of a 0.82 Bendix share for each share of Martin Marietta.

Upon receiving the letter announcing the offer just after 9 on Wednesday morning, August 25, Pownall contacted Rauth, who said, according to Pownall, "Hey, look, we've already made you CEO, and this is a CEO's job, so you do it your way and I'll do anything I can to support you; we only need one captain of this ship." Pownall added, "I'll tell you if he'd wanted to do it himself, I wouldn't have objected at all."

Pownall immediately called a special meeting. Although scattered across the country enjoying pre–Labor Day vacations, the directors and officers assembled the next day at headquarters for a briefing about the options management was considering for formal submission to the board. (See Figure 6.4 for a list of the directors.)

Figure 6.4
Board of Directors, Martin Marietta

Thomas G. Pownall, Chairman and CEO
Martin Marietta Corporation
Griffin B. Bell, Senior Partner
King & Spalding

Frank X. Bradley, President and CEO
Halco Inc.

John J. Byrne, Chairman and CEO
GIECO Corporation

A. James Clark, President and CEO
Clark Enterprises, Inc.

James L. Everett III, Chairman and CEO
Philadelphia Electric Company

Frank M. Ewing, Chairman and President
Frank M. Ewing Co., Inc.

William W. Hagerty, President
Drexel University

John Hanigan, Chairman
Genesco, Inc.

Charles Hugal, Executive Vice President
AT&T Corporation
(Mr. Hugal resigned from the board in September 1982
   after a job change created a conflict of interest.)

Melvin R. Laird, Senior Counselor
The Reader's Digest Association, Inc.

J. Donald Rauth, Chairman and retired CEO
Martin Marietta Corporation

David C. Scott, Chairman and CEO
Allis-Chalmers Corporation

Eugene M. Zuckert, Former Secretary
U.S. Air Force

Bendix's hostile move wasn't a complete surprise, because in October 1981, Rauth was told by a mutual acquain-
tance that William Agee wished to meet him for lunch. Agee
was Bendix's aggressive young CEO, and Rauth was instantly
suspicious. Believing Martin Marietta's stock was undervalued, Rauth was concerned that the lunch conversation might
involve a takeover proposal. He declined the invitation and
immediately organized a response team, which consisted of
Martin Marietta financial and legal personnel, as well as their
outside counterparts at the investment bank of Kidder, Peabody; the law firm Dewey, Ballantine, Bushby, Palmer &
Wood; and the investment relations firm Morrow & Company.
Later in October, a merger and acquisition specialist from Kid-

der, Peabody made a presentation to the board, showing why Martin Marietta might look attractive to another company: it had a sizable cash flow with which a predator could finance a takeover; 72.8% of its shareholders were institutional investors, who were more likely to sell during a takeover; and finally, two divisions, aluminum and cement, were in a slump, affecting the company's earnings and its stock price. Although the directors understood this vulnerability, the hostile tender offer was, nonetheless, a shock. After talking to Rauth, Pownall read Agee's letter to the response team, which began to evaluate the offer and to prepare a presentation to brief the board on August 26, because the directors would ultimately have to recommend whether or not shareholders should tender their shares.

With this background, at the first formal board meeting on August 30, the directors discussed whether or not to accept the Bendix offer and, if not, how to respond. Pownall asked Kidder, Peabody to give its evaluation of the offer. The Kidder, Peabody representative's first words were, "The Bendix offer is inadequate." He went on to say:

> A raider normally has to pay at least a 60% premium for control and Bendix has offered a premium of only 30%. Furthermore, Martin Marietta appears to be at the bottom of its earning cycle, but because it has just invested $1.6 billion in capital expenditures, it is in a very good position for recovery.

The Kidder, Peabody presentation lasted approximately two hours. Next, the Martin Marietta lawyers presented their analysis, advising the board that there were no strong legal impediments (such as antitrust issues) to the offer. Considerable discussion ensued between the board and its investment and legal advisers, and after roughly five hours, the directors felt they had considered all the alternatives. Rauth then called for a vote on the offer, which the directors unanimously rejected.

The second part of the meeting lasted another four hours and focused on a response to the rejected offer. Although Kidder, Peabody identified a number of possible responses, ranging from antitrust litigation to locating a possible white knight, it suggested that none of them would be in Martin Marietta's best interest, recommending instead a relatively unique alternative: a countertender. If Martin Marietta could borrow enough money, it could buy a controlling interest in Bendix. Because of a difference in the Delaware and Maryland corporation statutes, Martin Marietta could act more quickly to take control of Bendix. Under Maryland law, where Martin Marietta was incorporated, a company was required to call and conduct a shareholder meeting before a merger could be completed. The statute also stipulated that the company had to wait at least 10 and not more than 90 days after notifying the shareholders of the meeting before holding it. In Delaware, where Bendix was incorporated, there was no requirement for such a meeting. Instead, directors could complete a merger by consent voting unless prohibited by a corporation's charter, which was not the case at Bendix, so there was no excuse for a delay. Therefore, if Martin Marietta made the offer immediately, it could purchase the Bendix shares and oust its board at least four days before Bendix could do the same to them.

The Martin Marietta directors discussed the countertender alternative and decided that, if there were to be a merger of the two corporations, Martin Marietta's offer represented a better financial package for its shareholders than Bendix's. The board voted unanimously to tender for Bendix and approved a two-part offer, consisting of a $75 per share cash tender on the front end, and a package of securities with a lesser value on the back. The cash portion represented a 50% premium over market for the Bendix shares. The offer was designed to encourage the Bendix shareholders to tender immediately to Martin Marietta.

Once the board approved the countertender, Kidder, Peabody began contacting other corporations that might be interested in purchasing Bendix divisions. Kidder, Peabody hoped such divestiture would reduce Martin Marietta's debt burden if the deal went through. Harry Gray, CEO of United Technologies and a good friend of Pownall's, jumped at the chance. Dubbed the "Gray Knight" by a Wall Street takeover professional, he saw Martin Marietta's bid as an opportunity to acquire some of Bendix's major divisions, as well as a portion of their half-billion-dollar cash reserve, at a bargain price. United Technologies also decided to tender for Bendix at the same price. Pownall and Gray worked out an agreement whereby the two companies would, in effect, divide up Bendix depending on who ultimately purchased control. The tentative plan was that United Technologies would get Bendix's large automotive and industrial businesses, its pool of cash, and its portfolio of marketable securities. In return for $600 to $700 million, Martin Marietta would acquire all Bendix divisions that would present antitrust problems for United Technologies, such as aerospace and electronics, but that could be beneficial to Martin Marietta. The agreement was mutually beneficial. Not only did Wall Street analysts feel that the United Technologies offer gave Martin Marietta's bid greater credibility, the market seemed to, as well. After the agreement was announced, Bendix stock jumped $6 from $56.50 to $62.50 a share. United Technologies' shares increased from $47.125 to $48.50, and Martin Marietta moved from $35.63 to just $36 a share, well below the Bendix offer.

Even though Martin Marietta had lined up tenders for the majority of Bendix's outstanding stock, Pownall and the board didn't want to be forced to buy the shares unnecessarily. They were all aware that the deal could mean financial suicide for both companies. As the day drew near when Bendix could begin buying Martin Marietta shares, the directors became increasingly concerned that Agee was not convinced Martin Marietta's offer was credible. Griffin Bell explained, "It made sense to me. We said that we wanted to buy, but we were leaving seven ways to get ourselves out of it, so why should anyone believe that we really intended to go through with the deal?"

The board wanted to send a clearer signal to Bendix. On September 13, the directors voted to drop all but two of the seven conditions that had been appended to Martin Marietta's initial offer. Martin Marietta would now be obligated to purchase the tendered Bendix shares, unless the Bendix board either withdrew its offer, or passed shark-repellent provisions to its charter. The board assumed its decision to drop the conditions would convince Agee to back out, but events didn't unfold as anticipated.

On September 16, the Bendix board unanimously approved the purchase of the tendered Martin Marietta shares. Agee decided, however, not to limit his purchase to 50% of the

outstanding stock. He requested that the Bendix board au-
thorize an additional $400 million to increase Bendix's own-
ership to 70% of the Martin Marietta outstanding shares. He
believed that once Bendix owned 70% of Martin Marietta, its
board would give in. To safeguard his assumption that the
Martin Marietta directors would not proceed with the countertender, Agee offered to indemnify them for any liability they
might incur by deciding not to proceed.

Having waived all but two conditions to the Bendix offer,
Martin Marietta was contractually obligated to spend $892
million for 50.3% of Bendix's outstanding shares. The pros-
pect of financial suicide loomed large, and the board faced one
of the most challenging decisions of the takeover ordeal. If
Martin Marietta withdrew its offer to purchase the tendered
shares, the directors would risk breaking the law, under the
provisions of the Securities Exchange Act of 1934. In considering this decision, one director questioned, "Just who would
we be reneging on anyway? We would be reneging on the
arbitrageurs, not on the shareholders, because they were all
gone; they'd already sold out." Martin Marietta's outside
counsel, however, had a word of caution:

> There are some risks involved. The shareholders
> will definitely sue you and the company will probably
> owe hundreds of millions of dollars in reparations. Al-
> though the Bendix management did agree to indemnify
> you, there is a chance that a federal judge would decide
> that indemnification is not in the public interest which
> would mean that all of you would then be liable.

He also explained that although it was unlikely a judge would
rule in this fashion, it was possible, and advised the board
members not to withdraw.

The circumstances were clear. If Martin Marietta canceled
the offer, the two companies would not lose $2 billion in
equity, nor would they be left enormously leveraged. On the
other hand, if the directors voted to withdraw the offer, they
would risk significant civil liability. As the directors debated,
it became evident that the dangers of withdrawing the offer
outweighed the potential benefits of going ahead. The board
voted to proceed with their offer for the tendered 11.8 million
shares of Bendix.

On the afternoon of September 22, a director of the Allied Corporation called Pownall to inform him, "We've been talking to Agee and we think we've got a deal. Our board has agreed to buy Bendix and maybe you'd like to talk to Hennessey [the Allied CEO]." The Martin Marietta board waited for Allied's announcement, but it came so late in the day that the company still had to purchase the tendered Bendix shares. Nevertheless, Pownall and Ed Hennessey met to discuss the situation at 9 that evening. If Allied bought Bendix, Martin Marietta would own 50% of their new subsidiary, and Allied would own 70% of Martin Marietta. The two CEOs decided the prudent course was to work out a buy-back arrangement. Allied would purchase the Bendix shares not already owned by Martin Marietta, for a package of Allied stock and securities worth $85 a share, making Bendix a wholly owned subsidiary of Allied. Martin Marietta would then swap its stake in Bendix for an equivalent amount of its own stock. This would leave Allied with a 39% stake in Martin Marietta, which they agreed not to vote, buy, or sell for 10 years, as part of a "standstill" pact. It would cost Martin Marietta $917 million to buy its shares back from Bendix, and it would receive $862 million for the Bendix shares it owned. This arrangement was approved by the Martin Marietta board, and was the basis upon which the crisis was resolved.

In the 30 days during which the Martin Marietta board contended with Bendix's hostile takeover attempt, the company's debt-to-equity ratio increased from 25% to 80%, and its outstanding shares decreased from 36 million to 16 million. The corporation paid immense fees for the services of investment bankers, lawyers, and advertising media. Despite the costs, Martin Marietta remained an independent entity, and the directors believed they had fulfilled their responsibilities.

Directors' Assessment

Time Commitment

As the directors looked back at these events, they described how the challenges altered their normal role. The most obvious change was their increased time commitment. The Martin Marietta board met 12 times during the 30-day crisis, an obvious disruption of, and pressure on, directors' normal schedules. Some of the meetings were as long as nine hours, yet all accepted the commitment as part of their job.

As Melvin Laird described it:

> The climate was one of recognized urgency where all the directors knew the stakes were high and we wanted to do the best possible thing for the Martin Marietta Corporation. I did not feel the firm could just sit by and let some guy who was interested in a fast dollar come in and scramble everything up.

A crisis like this, with deadlines imposed by laws and regulations, with external actors, and with great media attention, puts directors in the spotlight, obliging them to sacrifice other activities to meet their responsibilities. This is a practical problem of governance that cannot be avoided. A balanced assessment of governance in such situations compels us to appreciate the willingness of directors like those at Martin Marietta to devote the time, regardless of personal or professional inconvenience, to deal with crises, particularly since their only significant compensation is a sense of accomplishment and personal learning.

Outside Advisers

While the extra time was manageable, directors viewed the increased reliance on outside experts as more complicated and came, retrospectively, to different conclusions. Frank Ewing told us: "I didn't think they should have swayed the other directors as much as they did, but the fact of the matter is that the other guys didn't really listen to each other; they listened to the outside advisers and then followed their advice."

Jack Byrne commented: "Despite good, solid conversations, the way I remember it is that by the time we would get around to voting, the technocrats would have constrained the options so much that you were almost always faced with a single alternative and I don't think I can remember a vote that wasn't unanimous. The technocrats just took 98% of the ball game right out of our hands."

Melvin Laird saw it differently. "The professionals were key players, but that's just what they were—professional consultants—not decision makers."

Opinions also differed about how to use the expert advice. At one extreme were those who believed the experts had a great influence because following their advice afforded legal protection. For example, Jack Byrne felt that the most important aspect of the sequence of events was

> . . . not necessarily how it all worked out; it was whether or not the directors did what the experts told them to do. If your lawyer says, "Do A," and you vote to do C, you automatically lose the defense of saying, "I was simply doing what my hired adviser said." You tell the judge, "I hired Goldman and Sullivan and Cromwell and advisers from both firms said this and I went along with it"; it is very, very hard for a judge to come back and say that you acted imprudently. But, if they told you to do this and you do something else, then you have sailed out of the safe harbor of having upheld your business judgment.

Griffin Bell felt that, in the future, he would deal with experts differently.

> I think we learned a lot about how to deal with investment bankers as a result of the takeover. None of us had had any experience with them and I think, if I had it all to do over again, I would have gone out and made them tell us exactly what the stock was worth. At least I would have done that, and I feel certain the other board members would have felt the same way. Investment bankers serve a good purpose, but they don't serve all purposes. The problem with investment bankers knowing more about what a company is worth than the people who run it is that they don't know anything about intangible values; they just know about a bunch of formulas. A company has got so many other things to consider in addition to sales.

Other directors felt less pressure to heed the experts' advice. For example, Melvin Laird:

> A director doesn't want to pay too much attention to the bankers and the attorneys. As I said before, they are there for their fees and their personal glory. You know you've got to be suspicious of these investment

*bankers; they know that the longer they're involved, the
higher their fees will be.*

Laird was also less concerned about the legal aspects: "I
felt if I were making the right decision, then it would definitely stand up in court."
Don Rauth agreed:

> *A director really has to do what he thinks is right.
> If I were ever called to the stand, I would want to testify
> that I had done what I believed was the best possible
> alternative given the time pressure we were all under. I
> listened to the consultants' presentations and asked the
> necessary questions, but when it came time to raise my
> hand aye or nay, I did what I felt was best.*

Two facts stand out in these comments. First, the outside
experts did influence the outcome, though, in retrospect, individual directors' opinions varied on how great their influence
was. Though the directors were the decision makers, the experts' advice had a major impact on the decisions of many of
them. Expert advisers, then, can threaten the board's power to
reach independent conclusions, but most striking is that the
directors didn't share their reservations about the advisers
during the board meetings. Given the time pressures, this is
understandable, but it's another example of how the failure of
board members to discuss underlying pressures can impair
their power to govern. In this instance, if the directors had
agreed about how to consider the experts' advice, and how to
deal with them, they would have felt less constrained. Perhaps
this matter should be discussed in advance of an actual crisis.

Board Accountability

The crisis also produced tensions about accountabilities.
Jack Byrne commented: "Talk about your chemistry; we all
knew why we were there, and so the first thing that happened
is that the directors shouted a pledge of allegiance to the shareholders' interests."
Melvin Laird was aware of the directors' traditional purpose when he said, "The board has got to place primary importance on the interests of the shareholder," but he recog-

nized broader responsibilities, too. "Employees come second, and management is a distant third. Personally, I feel that the employees are of critical importance because the shareholder is better protected if the employees are happy and have high morale—it's the only way a company can maximize its productivity."

When asked about this, Griffin Bell responded:

> We had the shareholders' interests in mind as number one. We also had other interests in mind, but they were things that you can't consider unless you consider them under the shareholders' interests. You can consider the employees and their feelings, because their morale has a lot to do with the company's overall success. You also have to be concerned about your top people who are in demand by other companies. You have to give them some form of golden parachute so you won't lose your brightest minds.

Tom Pownall was more pragmatic: "If the price had been adequate, we would have had to have sold it, even to someone we didn't like. We would not have had a choice if the deal had been good enough for our shareholders."

There was, however, a bias among the directors to ensure that the company remain an independent entity, if at all possible. According to Pownall, the board "basically and fundamentally did not like the management style that Agee used. It was nothing personal; we just didn't think it would be right for Martin Marietta."

Laird, too, reflected this view: "Martin Marietta could have been hurt if it had been taken over by Bendix, which had no experience in national security–related operations."

Byrne had another variation on the theme.

> We're not going to admit to ourselves that somebody else could run this place any better, even if it were true. There is always a bias toward the opinion that the organization is working right; after all, we're all managers and we know how to run things. Thus the board assumes that the company can, and should, stay together. The only time when that assumption becomes

an issue is when the price being offered is overwhelmingly greater than the present value of the future financial rewards that the management might get for the owners. Then there's no question; we'd have to sell.

Dealing with the Bendix offer caused a lot of soul-searching. For many directors, there must have been conflicting feelings about how to balance shareholder interests with other considerations. While these feelings apparently weren't discussed, it didn't seem to matter, probably because so many of the directors implicitly wanted the same thing—the survival of Martin Marietta as an independent entity. They achieved their goal, as it happens, in a way that also served the interests of the stockholders.

To accomplish it, they built a consensus around a strategy to scare Agee off. Although the vote to ratify the countertender proposal was unanimous, the directors had different expectations about how events would unfold. But, this time, because they had a concrete decision to make, they had discussed their differences.

Bell thought that Martin Marietta would be able to take control of Bendix because of the differing laws. He saw the strategy as "not just a Pac-Man defense, but a Pac-Man–plus scheme, where the plus was the fact that the takeover law in Maryland differed from the law in Delaware."

Laird also felt that Martin Marietta would prevail: "I really believed we would acquire Bendix at the price we were offering, because we were quite sure that the institutional investors would have to tender at the premium price we were offering."

Rauth shared Laird's view that "once we made the decision to buy the Bendix shares, we intended to buy them. It wasn't a ploy. We saw the countertender as the only way to remain an independent entity."

Ewing, on the other hand, was less confident. "I never thought that we'd ever own the Bendix shares. I felt it would be like one animal bleeding the other's veins in a tangled embrace. I thought Martin Marietta would eventually convince Agee to back down."

The directors, in retrospect, also disagreed about whether

or not they could be indemnified if they reneged. Don Rauth never thought that Martin Marietta could back out or that the board had any choice once it had offered to buy the shares:

> *It was incredible—Bendix's lawyers were telling us to break the law. They said that if we would agree to back out of our offer, which is the same as breaking a contract, they would indemnify us. It was ridiculous and I never, for an instant, paid any attention to it.*

Byrne, reflecting his broader responsibilities, was not quite as certain that the board should go by the book.

> *I actually argued along with one other director in favor of reneging. It was clearly in the nation's best interest that we not let all this money leave these two huge firms. How could we just let the two companies cave in to a black hole of enormous debt and risk going bankrupt? That clearly is not in the nation's best interest, and I really believed that a judge would have to uphold that. I guess the people on the Martin Marietta board, with a strong financial background, identified with this argument. The people who had a strong legal background, however, said, "Wait; we need to listen to our counsel before we commit ourselves to anything."*

As the directors dealt with specific decisions under extreme time pressures, they agreed on actions, without necessarily agreeing on the fundamental reasons for the actions or on the likely outcomes. Again, the lack of agreement on fundamentals didn't create a significant problem, and the board's power to govern wasn't really an issue, because it and the new CEO implicitly agreed that the independence of Martin Marietta was the desired outcome.

The Board and the CEO

What didn't change as the crisis unfolded was the board's normal relationship with its CEO. True, the new CEO was tested sooner than anyone would have expected, but once Chairman Rauth let Pownall run the show, the leadership problem was Pownall's. In assessing Pownall's performance after the event, the directors were complimentary. Bell described him as "a man who possessed all the manifestations of leadership that one would expect from an Annapolis graduate. He has vigor, he is articulate, and most of all he is intelligent." He went on to say:

> It takes a strong man to put up with an independent board. You have to have a lot of confidence in yourself. The weaker the leader, the less likely that he will surround himself with forceful directors, and the opposite, of course, is true, which applies to Tom.

Laird commented: "Although he was a new CEO who was just feeling his way around, he did a great job; he bent over backward to make sure that there were no secrets and that we had all the information we might need in order to draw intelligent conclusions."

Byrne concurred, saying that the CEO

> . . . made sure that his board never felt taken advantage of and that they had plenty of opportunity to say whatever they wanted. He encouraged contradictory views, all of which worked to make us feel part of the team. I am quite sure that because we all felt that we had been participants at every key decision stage, and because we knew we were not going to be constantly surprised, we all stuck by him through to the bitter end.

Although Pownall clearly took the leadership role, the directors felt that they played a critical part in making decisions. Rauth described the board as "a very professional group of people who were well balanced." Laird described his colleagues as "strong minds who were very good at asking the key questions at the right times." He felt that the board played a very specific part during the takeover.

> In these sorts of situations, the board can't let the management get too carried away. The management has got to run the show, but it can't careen around with it. It is essentially a checks-and-balances system, like Congress, where the management is the executive branch and the board is the legislative one.

In a clear external crisis, like this one, there is a natural tendency for the CEO and directors to unite. If the directors, as the Martin Marietta board did, have confidence in the CEO, he or she retains the leadership mantle. But since the board has increased exposure in such a situation, both legally and publicly, they want to be decision makers as well as advisers. Pownall obviously recognized this. He solicited his directors' opinions on essentially every issue and gave them plenty of information with which to make decisions. The directors, therefore, felt that they had the power to make the decisions affecting the company. Recalling the crisis, several directors drew a contrast with their peers at Bendix. Bell said, "Agee had his plan and he never got off it, even as the facts changed. We were obviously not dealing with a normal situation where people tend to act and react; he just never budged."

Byrne added:

> From what I understand, and I know some folks who were directors of Bill Agee's, their sense was that they were just being asked to ratify decisions that he had already made, and that they were part of the deal early on, but gradually he lost their confidence. For example, he fired one of the investment banks, Salomon Brothers, and hired somebody else without telling the board. I get the impression that there was just an enormous difference between the chemistry of the Martin Marietta board and that of Bendix's, during the whole thing. The most conclusive evidence is that, at the very end, when Agee needed his directors the most, they had a violent debate and four directors ended up walking out on him on the spot. That didn't happen by accident. That happened because Pownall and Agee had fundamentally different approaches and it turned out to be a very important fact because, in the end, Agee was left without any high ground and he didn't have any choices left.

Don Rauth also recognized the difference. "Bendix had an entirely different culture. Those of us on the board at Martin Marietta didn't really have egos; we just had practical concerns."

Conclusions

When Ed Hennessey from Allied stepped in and purchased Bendix, he appeared to be the only winner. Time, however, has shown that Martin Marietta has fared remarkably well. Byrne commented that "some financial people would say that the whole thing was the best thing that ever could have happened to Martin Marietta because it forced us to do a huge recapitalization. We shrank the equity, borrowed a lot of cash, and sold businesses that we shouldn't have been in. The shareholders who stuck with the company came out far, far better than they probably would have, had Bendix never made its bid. The Lord works in mysterious ways."

Those who argue that capital markets are the best means to discipline management will see Byrne's conclusion as support for their position. But these events are also evidence of the importance of capable directors in such situations. If the directors had not committed their time, intelligence, and effort so effectively during the month-long crisis, the outcome might have been different. Similarly, if Pownall had not had the wisdom to allow the board to share his power, and debate the complex issues, there might be a different and sadder conclusion for the Martin Marietta Corporation, its shareholders, and other interested parties.

One could argue that the Martin Marietta directors should have been more explicit with each other about their conflicting accountabilities, and how to utilize outside experts; however, this failing, if it can be called that, didn't impair their capacity to act: first, because they had an implicit agreement about their fundamental purpose, which they shared with Pownall; and second, while many things changed during the crisis, their reliance on the CEO as a leader did not.

Dunntech, Inc.

The second crisis we will examine was also sudden, in this instance internal; the unexpected death of the CEO. While less publicized than the Martin Marietta case, the events at this manufacturer of electronic equipment were no less traumatic for the company.

The Tragedy

At 8:00 A.M. on Monday, October 3, 1983, Marilyn Baker, secretary to John Barrow, CEO of Dunntech, received a call from Barrow's driver that Barrow had just been taken by ambulance to a hospital, suffering from what appeared to be a serious heart attack. Pale with shock, Baker rushed into the office of corporate secretary Peter O'Brien. O'Brien first called his own wife and asked her to go to Mrs. Barrow, then called the hospital, but since Barrow had arrived only within the hour, there was no news on his condition. O'Brien next called the company's medical director, Dr. Sheldon, who volunteered to go to the hospital, where he was on the staff, to see if he could help.

For the next hour O'Brien paced and quietly talked to Marilyn Baker. Both were still stunned since Barrow, at 46, had seemed in perfect health. A few minutes after 10, Dr. Sheldon telephoned with the tragic news that Barrow had succumbed to a massive coronary.

Baker knew from O'Brien's expression that the news was bad, and after regaining a semblance of composure she agreed to try to locate Gerald Marks, the chief financial officer, who was in New York. O'Brien called Robert Johnson, executive vice president of U.S. operations, who was in Honolulu at a sales meeting, and James Pritchard, executive vice president of international operations, who was still at home, having returned the evening before from Europe. Finally, he went down the hall to speak to the secretary of Joseph Garrison, executive vice president of manufacturing. After telling her the news, he asked her to try to reach Garrison, who was on a vacation cruise in the waters off Alaska. The message to all the executives, after telling them of the boss's death, suggested that they return to the company's California Silicon Valley headquarters as soon as possible, so that "they could begin to consider who was going to take Barrow's place."

This was especially difficult, since Barrow had been CEO for less than a year, having been appointed after the untimely death of the company's founder, Thomas Dunn, in November 1982. As O'Brien left Garrison's secretary, he considered what else needed to be done. Clearly, someone had to inform the company's employees and, of course, the board of directors. Since the directors were in O'Brien's direct purview, he called Wilson Ford, the company's longest-service director, to tell him of the tragedy and to seek his advice. (See Figure 6.5 for a list of the directors.)

Figure 6.5
Board of Directors, Dunntech, Inc.

Wilson Ford
Engineering consultant; retired director of a major electronics laboratory
Ralph Springer
Chairman and CEO of a computer company
Robert Johnson
Executive Vice President, Dunntech Corporation
Edward White
Independent investor and consultant
William Gerson, Ph.D.
Professor of physics at a major university
David Kolb
Professor of business
Robert J. Weiss
Private investor and trustee
Daniel Hare
CEO of an electronics company
C. Jackson Chase
Partner of Chase & Evans
Richard A. McFarlan
CEO of a software company

As he dialed Ford's number, O'Brien wondered how to break the news, since Ford had been close to both Dunn and Barrow, serving each not only as a technical consultant, but also as a confidant on many company issues. When he heard Ford's voice, O'Brien blurted out the news. It took Ford several minutes to recover. He then suggested he contact the other directors and get back to O'Brien with the board's wishes.

The Company

Dunntech, with 1982 sales of $1.2 billion, was the only major U.S. manufacturer of certain sophisticated switching equipment for the telecommunications and information-processing industries. Its three U.S. competitors were all small new ventures, still led by their engineer-founders. The company's major competitors were a division of a major European electronics firm located in Germany, and a large Japanese company. Most of the company's 7,000 employees were based in its three Silicon Valley manufacturing facilities, in its nearby R&D center, and in sales and service offices in the United States and Canada, as well as in major European and South American cities.

The Directors' Dilemma

By early afternoon Ford had reached only four of the ten outside directors, and had drawn three conclusions from his discussions with them. First, since the next regular board meeting was scheduled for the following Monday, there was no point in calling a special meeting before then. The directors he had talked to agreed to come in on Sunday evening, if necessary, expressed appreciation for his initiative, and encouraged him to contact the remaining directors.

Although all wanted time to think, their first reaction was that the successor should come from inside. They reasoned that few, if any, senior American managers were both knowledgeable about the company's products and markets, and had run a large company. They were also aware that since Barrow was young and apparently healthy, and had been CEO less than a year, the board had no succession plan. Therefore, Ford suggested that the management team meet to discuss who should lead the company.

Realizing that most of the senior officers were away, he called O'Brien and suggested that the latter arrange a meeting of Garrison, Johnson, Marks, and Pritchard as soon as possible. He explained:

> You all have a crucial role to play in this, because you are the ones who are going to have to run the com-

pany no matter what we (the directors) decide. Further, you will have to help all 7,000 of our employees recover from what has to be a tremendous shock.

In recalling the conversation later, Ford also remembered telling O'Brien that there was no guarantee that the board would accept their suggestions, but said he felt that for the directors to deliberate on a matter this serious, without input from management, would be a dereliction of duty. Ford explained his thinking to the other directors later that day, and the next. Thus, while there was no opportunity for the directors to discuss the issue together, none objected to Ford's plan.

After the fact, however, the directors had mixed feelings about senior management taking the initiative in determining who should be Barrow's successor. Ralph Springer reflected:

> *The management guys at Dunntech did something that I thought was truly unique. Without any direct intervention from the board, they took it upon themselves to discuss the situation and come up with a proposal for a new CEO. I thought it was a great tribute to John, and probably to Tom [Dunn, the founder], that the group would do that.*

William Gerson was similarly impressed.

> *I was vastly relieved, and it is not too strong to say delighted, that the management team did not fall apart under the strain of the situation. It was a wonderful thing that they got together and talked about the issue, because we were in a position to be supportive of something that management had already agreed upon. It would have been much harder for us to determine the successor if they had been unable to come to a consensus.*

David Kolb explained his thinking.

> *I thought Ford's plan was a sound one, because I had no doubt that management would select Bob Johnson, and I believed he was fully capable of doing the job and was our best bet. Furthermore, by letting the managers become involved, we assured their support of Johnson. I saw no risk in doing it this way.*

Daniel Hare, however, was less enthusiastic in retrospect, feeling "that the directors should have consulted among themselves first."

> I think that the board should have met in executive
> session to consider the alternatives, make a decision,
> and then cause whatever they concluded to happen.
> For the board to tell the residual management to sit
> down and decide how to divide the spoils was clearly
> an inappropriate way to handle the situation. If it
> turned out that the board did not agree with the man-
> agement's proposal there could have been a real
> conflict.

Management's Response

Unaware that they didn't have the board's unanimous support, the senior executives met the morning after the tragedy. A jet-lagged Johnson joined O'Brien at his home to begin formulating management's proposal. They considered various alternatives, beginning with the possibility of bringing in an outsider. That idea was quickly dropped because they felt that the search would take a lot of time and, according to O'Brien, "We were concerned that the stock market might lose some confidence in us if we didn't get someone at the helm quickly."

According to Johnson, he and O'Brien worked out "a relatively cockamamy scheme that identified Johnson as president and a committee of the board members as general overseers." Other top managers were to retain and/or expand their responsibilities. He recalled that, at the time, they were more concerned about keeping management happy and not offending anyone than they were about the plan's logic.

The next meeting of the day was held at headquarters, and the circle was enlarged to include Jim Pritchard, Dunntech's executive vice president, international; Gerald Marks, the chief financial officer; and Joseph Garrison, executive vice president, manufacturing. The three newcomers were "a little bent out of shape because they felt they had been kept outside of closed doors." For the first time, some dissonance surfaced.

When Johnson described the proposal he and O'Brien had

concocted, the tone abruptly shifted. Garrison, Marks, and Pritchard called the proposal ridiculous, and suggested that they come up with a more reasonable approach. Marks explained:

> We all took the position that said, "Look, from our perspective, the management is in a better position to know how to structure the company for optimal long-term stability. We should figure out right here which members of the management team belong where. A group of overseers from the board would just postpone decisions that probably shouldn't be postponed."

As the managers talked, a consensus quickly developed for Johnson to be CEO. Marks took himself out of consideration, saying: "I'm just a financial guy; we need someone with Bob's broad knowledge of the business to lead the company." Garrison concurred, adding that at age 62 he was looking forward to retirement in a couple of years. Pritchard, the youngest of the group at 37, was less forthcoming about his own motivations, although he enthusiastically endorsed Bob Johnson as CEO. Although Pritchard said nothing, the others were aware that he would be the most likely to succeed Johnson, in 10 years. The implicit question was how to broaden his experience, since he had been primarily involved in international marketing and, although technically trained, had little R&D or manufacturing experience. Johnson spoke up, suggesting that Pritchard become executive vice president of U.S. operations, a position involving not only oversight of U.S. marketing, which accounted for 70% of sales, but also research and product development. Everyone, including Pritchard, agreed. As Marks later said, "All of us, including Jim, understood that this position would give him the experience he needed to have the best shot at becoming Johnson's successor, and perhaps, as the company grew, to become chief operating officer."

With an agreement reached, Johnson suggested they discuss the idea with the individual directors before the board meeting. Since it would be embarrassing for Johnson to call, Garrison and Marks, being both older and better known to the directors, offered to make the calls.

Although most of the directors contacted before the formal meeting were enthusiastic about management's proposal, not every one was completely supportive. Springer told Marks that he didn't feel he knew Johnson well enough to vote for him. Springer had attended only one or two meetings as a director before Barrow's death, and felt there might be a better qualified candidate whom he did not know. Springer felt that the board was "casting a lot of concrete on an expedient solution, without really being certain that the management was making the best possible proposal." Springer decided to call Johnson. During their phone conversation, he said, "Please don't think I'm criticizing you, but I can't say now that I'm completely comfortable with your selection because I don't know you well enough. Although I know I will have to rely on the other directors' judgment, I'm really nervous about moving too far, too fast."

Other directors voiced a different concern, feeling uncomfortable about Pritchard becoming executive vice president, U.S. operations, because they didn't know him well enough, and because of his youth and lack of manufacturing and R&D experience. If, by another stroke of misfortune, Johnson died unexpectedly, they weren't sure Pritchard would be a fully competent CEO.

After Garrison and Marks had spoken with all the directors and understood their concerns, they met with Johnson again, but without Pritchard. Despite the concerns, Johnson felt he could make a persuasive case for Pritchard, and the rest of the meeting focused on how best to do that. They agreed not to speak to Pritchard, since nothing would be gained by letting him know of the board's lack of confidence.

The discussions among management and with individual directors had taken until Friday morning, October 7. At this juncture, Johnson called Ford to explain his thinking and to ask whether the board should meet Sunday night. Though unable to speak for other directors, Ford felt that the issue could be resolved on Monday, since all directors were aware of management's proposal.

Later the same morning, Daniel Hare, realizing there was no presiding chairman for the meeting, asked Ford if he would serve as acting chairman, if the other board members elected him. Hare felt Ford was the most logical candidate, because he lived in nearby Palo Alto, knew those involved, and was semiretired. Ford agreed to serve if elected and solicited Hare's thoughts about a special Sunday meeting. Hare agreed it wasn't necessary, adding, "If we need more time we can always continue Monday night, since the others can't fly back east until Tuesday morning."

Selecting a New Management Team

At the Monday board meeting, the first move was to elect an acting chairman. Hare nominated Ford, Ford accepted, and the rest of the board approved. Johnson was then asked to present management's proposal. He first explained that the management team considered only inside candidates because there was no fast and efficient way to locate qualified outside leaders, in an industry where there were no large U.S. competitors and where the technology and its application were so complex.

Johnson next noted that the recommendation included no titles but, because the bylaws specified the company needed a CEO in order to carry out certain specific responsibilities, he would take the job. Pritchard would be the executive vice president, domestic operations, and the other senior executives would divide up the remaining tasks. After the presentation, the management members left the outside directors to discuss the proposal. Most directors were comfortable appointing Johnson as president and CEO, but there were still reservations about Pritchard's appointment.

Some directors, however, felt there should be an outside search for a more experienced CEO. O'Brien, who attended as corporate secretary, recalled one board member pointing out that Dunn had spent years training Barrow to become the CEO and had expected to oversee Barrow's progress for at least four years during the transition period. Without Dunn or Barrow, this director felt that the lack of a top-level executive with lengthy exposure to the company's long-term strategy might threaten the corporation's future stability. He believed a more experienced outsider would ameliorate the problem.

According to Ford, the directors then discussed potential

outside candidates, but, as he recalled, "The more we talked about potential candidates, the more the list proved to be ridiculous. The directors quickly realized that time and availability were critical factors and we decided to consider Johnson's proposal, rather than quibble about possible outsiders." But the concerns about Pritchard remained.

When Johnson returned, they voiced those concerns, but Johnson assured them that he had great confidence in Pritchard, and the only alternative was an outside search; which was not likely to be fruitful. Further, if the board finally selected Pritchard after such a search, Johnson's and the board's relationship with Pritchard would have been damaged by that lack of confidence.

The board was in an awkward position. Johnson was making it clear that the righthand man he wanted was one with whom not all directors felt comfortable. Ford recalled:

> I wasn't quite sure what to do. I didn't know Jim well enough to approve the nomination enthusiastically, but I got a sense that the management meetings might have been a little rockier than they appeared on the surface, and Johnson was pushing Pritchard for a reason. I guess my reaction to this was that if a newly appointed CEO wanted someone strongly enough, I didn't see any reason not to go along, and I felt pretty strongly that, if it turned out to be a bad idea, we could take action and remove him. I also was under the impression from Dave Kolb, who apparently knew Pritchard quite well, that he thought very highly of him. Quite frankly, I put considerable stock in Dave's judgment.

Despite the potential difficulties, the board members approved Pritchard's appointment but, according to one director, they agreed only "as an expression of support for Johnson."

Making the Transition

Having determined who would fill the top management positions, ensuring a smooth transition was the board's next priority. Springer described the board's thinking:

> Because some very junior people were being asked
> to step into some top-level positions, far earlier in time
> than anyone had anticipated, it was the board's respon-
> sibility to play a more substantial role in supporting
> and aiding management. We were dealing with a new,
> green management that was stepping into a very com-
> plicated situation, without the needed preparation, and
> we needed to make sure it would be done right.

The first suggestion was the formation of an executive
committee of local board members who would meet with
Johnson once a week to provide advice and assistance. Three
board members, however, vehemently opposed the idea, worried that such a structure might create a two-tiered board,
consisting of the players and the "real" players. Johnson, and
some other directors, also felt an executive committee might
become too involved in the management of the firm. Ford
commented that "a board that degenerates into a management
committee is writing a prescription for disaster."

The Presiding Director

Someone then suggested that the board elect one of its
members as chairman, an idea that was ill received because it
might imply that the board had only limited confidence in the
newly appointed CEO. Springer then suggested electing a
"presiding director," from among the board members, to work
with the new management and ensure sufficient advice and
assistance from the directors. Ford liked the idea because he
felt outsiders would correctly infer from the title that the arrangement was only temporary.

After agreement to establish the position, the next question was, Who would fill it? Ford was the logical choice. When
asked, he agreed to serve and was unanimously elected presiding director. Despite the general enthusiasm about Ford's new
position, some directors still expressed concerns. Gerson wondered whether the presiding director should have an office at
headquarters, and would such an arrangement tempt him to

breathe down Johnson's neck? He also wondered how much Ford should be paid. The salary would have to compensate him adequately for the additional effort, without encouraging him to remain in the position too long. The directors suggested that Gerson discuss his concerns with Johnson and Ford, and that the three should determine the logistics of the job and decide on a fair salary. Working together, the three men came up with a plan, which was later approved by the whole board.

In January 1985, the board voted to promote Johnson to chairman, and the position of presiding director was eliminated. Dunntech, despite the tragic deaths of two chief executive officers, remained a stable and profitable corporation.

An Assessment

When asked to evaluate the board's performance through the crisis, directors responded favorably. Ford admitted there

> . . . were certainly things the board might have done that it did not, but most of those things were of secondary importance. One of the key reasons that the outcome was so positive was that the board didn't become factionalized. It never lost sight of its most important concerns: the shareholders' interests, the employees' security, and the community. I believe this unity was critical. I think that on an absolute scale, I would give the board's performance a B or even an A. Compared to other boards with which I have been involved, I would have to give the Dunntech board an A+.

O'Brien also felt that the board played a critical role in the resolution of the crisis. "The board responded nobly and, from the management's point of view, the board did all we could possibly have hoped. They were very supportive and they were careful to consider all of management's opinions. Most boards and top managements don't tend to see eye to eye, but that is certainly not the case here. I feel fortunate to have had the opportunity to get to know such an impressive group of people."

Assessments from those involved in tragic events are

bound to have a bias. From the perspective of directors and
management alike, the crisis was resolved in a manner that
sustained Dunntech, which was the outcome they all desired.
However, for those interested in how boards can deal more
effectively with crisis, the end result is not the only consideration. Of greater interest is how the directors dealt with the new
conditions the crisis produced.

From this perspective, the Dunntech board faced different
issues from those of its counterparts at Martin Marietta. In
dealing with an externally imposed threat, the latter had to
contend with outside experts, questions of accountability, and
intense time pressures. But there was an important constant, a
familiar relationship with the CEO. At Dunntech, in contrast,
the untimely death of the CEO created a leadership void not
only in the company, but also on the board. Further, the board
had to deal with the matter of its power versus that of management to control the succession questions.

Board Leadership

The matter of board leadership was resolved with the
selection of Ford as acting chairman. It was an easy choice
because he had been a long-service director, respected by his
peers and by management. He had been close to both deceased
CEOs, knew management as well as any other director did,
and he had time to do the job, although there is no evidence
that the situation took up an unusual amount of his or the
other directors' time. Further, Ford had asserted himself as a
leader as soon as Barrow's tragic death occurred. Finally, there
were no contentious issues to divide the board into factions.
Ford's leadership was readily accepted. If other directors objected, they said nothing either at the time or after the fact.

The Board's Power

Ford's suggestion that management meet to develop its
own solution, though well meant, had the unintended effect of
diminishing the board's power, already limited because of the
directors' dependence upon the remaining top managers. Even
if the directors had chosen to search for an outsider, or to

name one of their number as CEO, they had to retain the enthusiasm and commitment of the present managers.

It is also likely that, even without Ford's suggestion, management would have developed its own solutions. It had ample incentive to do so, since psychologically Dunntech's top managers considered the company their own and wanted to protect it. Further, they did not want an outsider as CEO.

Nevertheless, Ford's suggestion legitimized management's actions. Also, the directors, though in telephone contact with Ford, took no initiative to meet until their normal meeting, one week after the tragedy. While this may have been a practical decision, the signal to management was clearly that it had a week to come up with its own recommendations. Reading the situation this way, management contacted directors individually to test their reactions.

Apparently two directors were unhappy with the scenario—one was new, and didn't know Johnson well, and the other wanted the board to be more active. However, the only open dissension at the board meeting was about the possibility of selecting an outsider and the problem of naming Pritchard as number two. This is another example of directors' tendency to avoid sensitive issues. In this case, the directors' failure to mention their objections helped management seize the initiative.

The matter of Pritchard's position clearly demonstrates how limited the board's power was. Facing a unified management team and wanting Johnson to be CEO, the directors had little choice but to accept his recommendation. Johnson and the management team had the real power to force the issue.

What could the directors have done differently? Most important, they could have quickly convened a special board meeting, indicating that they were in charge and, as directors, intended to develop the process by which the next CEO would be selected. The message to management would have been clear: "The board has the power. If you want to develop your own ideas, that's fine, but we will decide." Under the circumstances, the outcome would likely have been the same, but it would have enabled the board to explore every option and to use its members' talents to find the best solution.

While critical of the board's abdication of power, a balanced analysis must also give credit for their innovative approach to retaining oversight over the new young management team. Electing a presiding director worked well, and is an idea we believe to be relevant for other companies, given the prevailing U.S. attitude toward not separating the role of chairman from that of CEO. Such a separation, which exists in just over 50% of public companies in the United Kingdom, is mistrusted by top managers and investors in the United States.[1] As the Dunntech directors concluded, investors may see it as a lack of confidence in the CEO. Many CEOs are also concerned that the chairman's position would be filled by their predecessor, thus complicating the jobs of leading their companies.

Recognizing these attitudes, the Dunntech directors had to find a way to gain the power of oversight over the new CEO. Their new CEO had less than ideal experience, yet they didn't want the investment community to perceive a lack of confidence in him. They were also aware of the fine line between directors' oversight of management and interference in management's prerogatives. The idea of a presiding director resolved these issues, putting in place, temporarily, an outside director who would counsel and observe the new CEO, while keeping the other directors informed. The directors got the control they wanted, Johnson didn't feel any undue interference, and the outside world probably never knew about the decision.

Power in Sudden Crises

If the power to govern is the essence of governance, our examination of these two crises reveals different problems for the boards. At Martin Marietta, even though Pownall was new, he was able with the support of his predecessor to maintain the existing power balance between the board and the CEO. It was, rather, the outside advisers who threatened the directors' power. In contrast, the sudden loss of the CEO at Dunntech created a vacuum that, unless the board established its leader-

---

1. Private conversation with director of Promotion of Non-Executive Directors (PRONED).

ship and controlled the selection process, diminished the directors' power.

The latter situation is common during internal crises, where the board often finds itself in positions critical of, and contrary to, the actions of the CEO and other top managers. Thus, in spite of the hoopla over takeovers and LBOs, we believe internally generated crises present directors with the greater challenge.

While the two cases were different from each other, they shared a similarity—both events were sudden and both boards had no doubt they had a crisis on their hands. Though directors sometimes disagreed on how to resolve the crisis, they shared a common purpose that united them around the need to act. As we examine two companies faced with gradual crises, we shall understand the importance of this simple fact.

Chapter 7

Resolving Gradual Crises

Sudden crises, though dramatic, may have less impact on the well-being of the U.S. economy than crises that are gradual, longer-lasting, and less sensational. For example, the scaling down of production in the American steel industry, spanning more than a decade, caused significant changes in shareholder value, employment rates, entire communities, and the U.S. balance of trade. Changes in the consumer electronics, automotive, chemical, and oil industries are other examples.

Gradual declines are a tremendous challenge to directors, as the Burlington Northern and Harvest cases illustrate. Directors and managers alike have trouble recognizing that a series of specific, year-to-year failures adds up to a long-term trend, and tend to view each event as independent and temporary, or cyclical. Recognizing the pattern in such trends is even harder for time-pressed directors, depending as they do on the CEO and management for information.

Another problem in handling long-term crises is that, inevitably, they involve a failure of management, usually including the CEO, and complicate the relationships among managers and between managers and directors. As the Harvest case illustrates, a long-term internal crisis is probably the most difficult situation a board can face. We begin, however, with the Burlington Northern Company, because its case typifies the difficulty directors face in a gradually declining industry.

Burlington Northern Corporation

Introduction

Historians often refer to the United States from the 1850s to the 1920s as the "steamcar civilization." In the mid-1870s an estimated 90% of all commerce between the West and the East moved by rail. One hundred years later, however, conditions in the railroad industry had drastically changed. In 1967, trucking overtook railways in terms of net operating revenues, and, in the same year, airplanes transported four times more passengers than trains did.[1]

Although major changes continued in the railroad industry through the 1970s, senior managers of the large lines were slow to respond. Their reluctance to act—because they were so emotionally wedded to railroading traditions—was one reason why the profitability of railroads continued to decline.

Burlington Northern's Traditions

It was precisely this scenario that the directors of Burlington Northern Company confronted in the late 1970s. Burlington Northern stood out among U.S. railroads because it not only operated more miles of track than any other, it was second only to the U.S. government in total land holdings, having been founded as a land-grant railroad. Despite immense real estate assets, top management and directors had always considered the company a railroad, rather than a natural resources or real estate company. (See Figure 7.1 for a list of the directors.)

Figure 7.1
Board of Directors, Burlington Northern Corporation

Royal D. Alworth, Jr., Chairman of the Board
Oneida Realty Company
Daniel P. Davisson, President
U.S. Trust Company of New York

---

1. Historical Statistics of the United States. (Washington, D.C.: Bureau of the Census, 1975), p. 708.

W. John Driscoll, President
Green Valley Holding Company

Mary Garst, Cattle Manager
The Garst Company

Pemberton Hutchinson, Executive Vice President
Westmoreland Coal Company

Norman M. Lorentzsen, CEO
Burlington Northern Company

Louis W. Menk, Chairman of the Board
Burlington Northern Company

Paul L. Parker, Executive Vice President
General Mills, Inc.

Bruce M. Rockwell, Chairman of the Board
The Colorado Trust

Gerald C. Ryan, President
Ryan Potato Company

Robert B. Wilson, Chairman of the Board
Weyerhaeuser Company

According to Paul Parker:

> For the most part, Burlington's perception of itself
> as a railway was reinforced by the company's location
> in St. Paul, Minnesota. James J. Hill's giant edifice was
> just down the street from the corporate headquarters.
> The artwork in the hallways depicted scenes from along
> the tracks, and our public affairs stance focused en-
> tirely on the railroad. Even in the boardroom, we sat
> under giant portraits of the great railroad moguls.

The railroad heritage was shared by senior managers,
most of whom had been "on the lines" for anywhere from 10
to 30 years. Bruce Rockwell described these men as

> . . . professional railroaders who, for the most part, had
> had very little experience outside of the industry. There
> was a mind-set that comes from working in the business
> that is single-minded, bureaucratic, and sometimes ar-
> rogant. These were not men of vision, unless it was tun-
> nel vision.

Robert Wilson recalled: "The first thing the president did every morning was read the derailment report. He was probably very effective at keeping the tunnels clear of snow, but he just had no concept of how to run an organization."

The CEO—Lou Menk

Burlington Northern's CEO in the 1970s was Lou Menk, a man whose early experience paralleled that of other top company officials, though his later career did not. In 1936, at the age of 19, he began as a messenger for the Union Pacific. Four years later he was hired by the St. Louis–San Francisco Railway Company as a telegrapher and worked there for the next 24 years, becoming chairman and president, in 1960, at the age of 44. Because he was approximately 10 years younger than the average railroad president, the eyes of the industry focused on him, and his peers considered him "the young upstart." Trade journals and business publications wrote profiles about him and, although he had little formal education, he was awarded numerous honorary degrees, as well as a Horatio Alger Prize.

Five years later, in 1965, Menk accepted the presidency of the Burlington Lines and, in 1966, he was asked to assume the same position at the Northern Pacific railroad. In 1969, Northern Pacific merged with the Burlington and the Great Northern, to form the Burlington Northern Company. Menk was elected CEO of the combined railroad, which became the nation's largest railway in terms of total road miles.

Menk's unusual career, according to Burlington directors, was attributable to his unique personality. Hutchinson characterized Menk as "big in every sense of the word. He's big physically, he's bighearted, and he's a big thinker." Parker described him as a man with

> . . . the most open mind of nearly anyone I have ever met. He doesn't worry much about whether or not the train line to Fargo has favorable operating ratios; he is more concerned about society at large. Nothing in economics, political science, or the fabric of the nation is beyond his field of interest. He is the only man I know who has ever moved from a yardmaster to a captain,

actually a general, of industry in such a short period of time.

Davisson described Menk as "a brilliant man for whom I have infinite respect. He's one of the nicest men who has ever lived, and he spreads his charm in every direction. He should probably have been a senator."

With such experience and personality, Menk was well equipped to head the three merged railroads. Unfortunately, the task was complicated by the oil crisis in the early 1970s and the continuing decline in the railroad industry. In 1972, the nation's freight trains covered 451,032 miles, whereas a decade later they traveled only 344,936 miles, and, from 1960 to 1980, passenger rail travel declined 49%.[2] Burlington Northern's railroad was also having its problems. While corporate return on equity in 1979 was 8.7%, the railroad division's return on average net investment was only 3.8%, which, according to the 1979 Annual Report, was "still substandard." While more money was invested in the railroad division than in any other, its profitability was lower than that of the rest.

The Directors' Responses

In 1975, the directors voted to reduce the cash dividend by 47%, from $1.60 to $0.85, thus publicly signaling their concern about railroad profitability. With this decision, the directors and officers realized they would need to explore a shift in the company's focus from the railroad to natural resources. Parker recalled another board member having pointed out at the time that "Burlington Northern was really not a railroad, but a natural resource company with a railroad running through it." Davisson remembered becoming increasingly concerned about the railroad's financial situation.

What I noticed, and what worried me, was that we were putting 90% of the capital into the railroad and were getting only 10% of the return from it. From 1970 to 1979, we spent $2.7 billion on the railroad division

2. Association of American Railroads, *Railroad Facts* (Washington, D.C.: 1987), p. 23.

*of the company but continued to have a substandard
return on equity.*

In 1979, the railroad contributed 81% of consolidated corporate revenues of $3.25 billion, but only 23% of corporate
pretax income of $175.4 million. Davisson, like other direc-
tors, was anxious to ameliorate the situation.

> *In looking at the company, I couldn't see anyone in
> the top levels of management who looked as though he
> could do the job. Furthermore, the board was made up
> of quite a few old-time railroaders from communities
> located along the track. They looked at the income from
> natural resources as a godsend that could finance addi-
> tional railroad expenditures that might eventually lead
> to a turnaround. I was a little different from the other
> directors in that I tended to look at the business as a
> whole and I didn't get too sentimental about it.*

Thus many directors, as well as top managers, viewed the
decline as temporary, a view that isn't surprising given their
heritage and their reliance on management for information. As
evidence of the difficulty of facing up to gradual deteriora-
tions, we emphasize that this particular decline had been evident for almost a decade before the directors took action—and
it was fortunate that some directors, less emotionally committed to railroads, recognized the difficulties as acute. Foremost among them was Davisson, who, because of his banking
background, had a broader and more realistic perspective than
some of the others. Davisson's inclination was to seek a top
manager who would make the necessary changes because he,
like many other directors, believed the best way to achieve
strategic change was to replace top management. Events soon
gave him the opportunity to act.

Menk's Retirement

In 1978, Lou Menk told the board he planned to phase
himself out of the business on a day-to-day basis, but wished
to retain the title of chairman. Menk explained: "My wife was
gravely ill and, after 16 years as CEO of four different railroads, I was getting a little tired of doing the same old thing."

After his sixtieth birthday, Menk appointed Norman Lorentzsen, 62, president and chief executive officer, pending the board's approval. Because Lorentzsen was two years older than Menk, board members felt that they still needed to identify a long-term successor. Furthermore, according to Bruce Rockwell, "As soon as Norm took over, we began running into problems of leadership, delegation, and personal relationships, so it became clear quickly that we would need to locate the next CEO."

Locating a Successor

At the time of his announcement, Menk himself had asked the board's personnel committee to address the longer-term succession issue, and Parker, a member of the committee, described the process. "First thing we did was look in the ol' refrigerator to see what was at arm's reach before going to find something at the store." The committee spent a great deal of time evaluating the available talent because, as Parker recalled:

> The entire board was predisposed to go inside. We didn't want to admit that we hadn't done our job in lining up the next CEO, one of the board's principal responsibilities. Unfortunately, in comparing the insiders at Burlington Northern to Lou Menk, the committee realized that there was no one there with either the breadth of knowledge or interest that could come close to Lou's.

Hutchinson had similar recollections:

> We discovered, however, that each [inside] candidate we evaluated lacked something. They were all over 50 and had been career men with the company from the start. It seemed that their outlooks were just too narrow to follow a man like Lou.

The committee met 6 times, over 18 months, before making a series of presentations to the full board, and the directors gradually understood that guiding the company into the next century necessitated an outside successor. According to Driscoll, "That decision didn't just jump in from out of the blue overnight; it was a slow realization that hit various board members at different times."

Davisson was the first director to express concern but, as he put it, "I was very careful not to lead any kind of palace revolt." He chose to talk to some of the board members individually and, as he said, "For the most part, they didn't disagree with me, but I don't think they wanted to upset any applecarts. I realized that if anything was going to happen, I would probably have to be the one to grab Lou's attention, which I ultimately did."

Davisson is pointing to the difficulties a director faces in taking the initiative in a crisis. Wanting to assert himself, he must do it carefully. The "applecart" to which he referred was the existing relationship between the directors and their popular CEO. Given their liking and respect for Menk, as well as boardroom norms, the other directors were reluctant to speak out.

Because of the barriers to open discussion, Davisson raised his concerns privately with Menk. He recalled:

> I didn't really have to fight very hard; all I did was turn the key in his mind. I think he had already realized that this man Lorentzsen was not right for the job and that everything could have fallen apart if he stayed in place too long. I just went to him and said that I didn't think his successor existed within the firm and that we should begin to look outside.

Menk concurred:

> It was after those talks that I came to realize Burlington Northern needed a generalist to run the place: someone who knew finance, who had had some operating experience, and who knew how to develop the resource end of the business. I realized the company had a lot of good railroad men, but the company needed someone with a little something more.

Menk also gave credit to Davisson:

> Danny Davisson had more to do with it than anyone or anything else. We had numerous rump sessions on airplanes during which he explained to me why he

*felt Burlington Northern needed a man who could man-
age a diverse corporation in a changing industry. After
one particular conversation, I went home and thought
about the situation quite a while and decided to hire
Booz, Allen & Hamilton to help identify potential candidates.*

What stands out in this account is how easily the problem
was dealt with once Davisson talked to Menk. It causes us to
wonder to what extent the delay and difficulty directors have
in dealing with such issues result from their own inhibitions.
More open and earlier discussion would certainly lead to
more effective governance.

The consultants located five possible contenders, one of
whom was Richard Bressler from Atlantic Richfield Corporation, with whom Menk sat on the General Mills board. Menk
interviewed several candidates, and then members of the personnel committee interviewed those whom he liked. Rockwell
was surprised that "the whole process moved with such re-
markable speed. We had it narrowed down to two or three
candidates in about three months." Ultimately Menk and the
directors agreed that Bressler was the best candidate and offered him the position.

Some directors were surprised that Menk had changed his
mind so quickly. Hutchinson commented:

*I have to give Lou Menk an awful lot of credit for
considering an outsider. Here he is, a railroad man all
his life, watching us reject one of his own people. In a
sense he was saying to the world, "I guess I haven't
fulfilled one of my primary responsibilities by not leaving a legacy of trained people to take over after I
leave." It must have been quite a blow for him.*

The board was also surprised by his choice. According to
Hutchinson, Dick Bressler

*. . . is about as different from Lou Menk as you can pos-
sibly imagine. He's urbane and refined, and Menk is
6'6" and rawboned, like a cowboy. Bressler wears tai-
lored suits and is a real professional manager type.
Menk rides horses on his ranch and is a real outdoors-*

man. We used to have steak and potatoes at the board lunches and now we're served fish and salad. It really fascinated me that Menk would pick this guy.

Despite their differences, Bressler was well suited to the challenges. According to Rockwell, Bressler "had a track record of being a very decisive, tough-minded numbers man who had had a variety of experiences." His career began at General Electric in 1952, where he worked for 16 years before leaving to become senior vice president at American Airlines. In 1973, he became senior vice president and later president of Atlantic Richfield Company. Bressler's background in natural resources and transportation meshed well with both Menk's and the board's hopes for Burlington Northern's future.

Changes under Bressler

Bressler came to Burlington Northern with a carefully conceived turnaround strategy and new ideas on how to utilize his board. His first priority was to balance earnings because, as he put it, "We can't have the transportation division dominating the rest of the business." To buttress the natural resource branch, Bressler's first move was to take over the El Paso Natural Gas Company in Texas. For this billion-dollar decision, the board was given ample material on El Paso's past and projected performance, as well as information about both the industry and competition. Furthermore, the board was asked to meet frequently for strategic discussions, before the decision was finally made to go ahead.

Bressler's second action was to move corporate headquarters from the Twin Cities, where the Burlington Northern's oldest division had been founded in 1856, to Seattle. In a situation unlike that of the first decision, the directors were given little information before the meeting and the subject was discussed for only two hours. Bressler told the board that he didn't like the tax structure in Minnesota, and that the headquarters of a transportation company didn't belong in the middle of the country. Thus, on the key strategic decisions, Bressler involved the board a great deal, but on less strategic decisions, board involvement was less.

Bressler also changed the nature of the board meetings.

According to Parker:

> The board meetings are a lot simpler than they
> were under Lou. He [Bressler] eliminated many of the
> traditional matters such as the listing of each land
> lease executed during the last month. Although it was a
> big waste of time, it had been done at every meeting
> since the Great Northern line was founded. No one ever
> thought to remove it from the agenda before.

Davisson described some other changes: "The presentations to
the board are now superb. They are now one-tenth as long as
they used to be, and they are about three times clearer. In
addition, they've cut down the number of meetings, and the
meetings themselves are now much shorter."

Directors also mentioned style differences between Menk
and Bressler. Hutchinson described Menk as

> . . . filled with tender loving care and warmth. He asked
> after your wife and remembered the names of your kids,
> making the boardroom seem like an extended family.
> With Bressler it's entirely different. There are no phone
> calls and the meetings are fewer and farther between.
> He has the attitude that "if you don't like what I'm do-
> ing, then get rid of me." Furthermore, he made it clear
> that the company was always for sale. He had no fear
> of being taken over.

Parker said:

> Menk's relationship with the board was excellent.
> He never talked down to his board and he always
> wanted to tap the resources of his directors' minds.
> Bressler is a good guy who is not exactly the type to
> reach out to his board for an opinion or for anything
> else. I think that is sort of a mistake—he's missing
> something.

Robert Wilson agreed: "Dick doesn't understand how useful a
board can be. He doesn't make any effort to cultivate his
board."

Nonetheless, after Bressler's first five years, Burlington
Northern was better positioned for growth, and financially

more stable. Between 1980 and 1984, operating revenues increased 131%, from $3.9 billion to $9.1 billion, whereas during the five-year period before Bressler, revenues increased only 102%, from $1.6 billion to $3.2 billion. The directors, in spite of some reservations, reviewing figures that revealed noteworthy financial gains, gradually agreed that the decision to look for an outside CEO had been sound. In five years, the company made a successful transition from a railroad to a natural resources company, in both a real sense and in terms of the public's perceptions.[3] Nevertheless, a few board members missed the old days. One commented: "The board meetings used to be fun, primarily because of all the traditions, and the way that Lou treated all of us. I think that Bressler's done a fine job in changing Burlington Northern, but it just isn't the same."

This is an appropriate comment with which to end because, as we have seen, the traditions about which this director nostalgically speaks were a major reason for both directors' and managers' slow response to the gradual crisis. Directors are no more immune to strongly held strategic beliefs than are top managers.[4] During the 1970s, when the country's railroads were obviously in an irreversible decline, the Burlington Northern board members failed to see what was happening because they considered themselves directors of a railroad, a vital industry the permanent decline of which was unthinkable. Thus, directors not only depend on management for objective information, they share emotional commitments and biases, which lead them to interpret data in a manner similar to the way management does.

In an evolving crisis there is no sudden event to dispel deeply held beliefs, unlike the Dunntech tragedy, where directors abandoned beliefs about how much experience a CEO needed, and Martin Marietta's crisis, when directors quickly

---

3. In June 1988, however, the company announced a restructuring plan that involved spinning off its natural resources operations. The announced reason, according to analysts, was to rid itself of large legal liabilities and claims pending against a subsidiary in the natural resources business, El Paso Natural Gas (*New York Times*, June 3, 1988, p. D 16).

4. Gordon Donaldson and Jay W. Lorsch, *Decision Making at the Top* (New York: Basic Books, 1983).

shed beliefs about the appropriate level of corporate debt. A clear crisis is a rallying point around which directors can assemble their collective power, but without a triggering event, change is more difficult to accept and initiate, and other means have to be found to coalesce group power. Consequently, directors like Davisson at Burlington Northern deserve a great deal of credit for assuming leadership and for daring to stray from the established order. Without such skillful and tenacious directors, gradual crises could continue until a company is mortally wounded. This is precisely what happened at Harvest. In this case, the missing ingredient was the emergence of active board leadership.

The Harvest Corporation

In 1973, The Harvest Corporation, a New England manufacturer of athletic and leisure shoes, reported record earnings. Net income had increased 25% over 1972 (from $67 million to $84 million), and the company increased its dividends 75% over the prior year. In the next four years, however, the company faced increased competition in the U.S. market and, in spite of tight control of costs and inventories, profits declined. In the 1977 Annual Report, management blamed economic conditions, saying: "Earnings for the year were disappointing to management due to increased . . . competition in the U.S. market. Furthermore, retailers had reacted to the influx of products by reducing their inventory levels of domestic products thereby shifting more of the burden to U.S. manufacturers."

Although increased competition had a severe impact during this period, it was not the only problem facing the company. During the 18 months from June 1976 to December 1977, the relationship between the chairman and former CEO, Charles Ward, and his successor, Robert Dalton, deteriorated. What had once been a father-son relationship turned into public hostility, distracting management and directors from the fundamental question of how to improve the company's financial and market performance.

Dalton's Selection

Before Ward's and Dalton's relationship soured, the two had been close for over 30 years. An outside director described Dalton's relationship with Ward as "a very intimate affiliation. Bob was his boy, his protégé."[5] Dalton recalled the early years with Ward similarly. "Charlie and I worked together throughout my career; I would regularly sit down with him and tell him what I was doing and what I was planning to do. He taught me a great deal and, in effect, he treated me as if I were the son he never had."

In less than 12 years, Dalton rose from chief industrial engineer to executive vice president, largely because of his success in improving manufacturing efficiency, even as the product line was broadened.

In the mid-1960s, after serving as CEO for over 20 years, Ward began looking for a successor. Since the company's traditional strength was in manufacturing, Dalton was obviously a prime candidate. But another senior executive at the time, the senior vice president of marketing, Paul Whitney, had reservations: "Dalton's ambition, from day one, was to be chief executive officer no matter what it took." He remembered workers in the New Hampshire plant who quoted Dalton as saying, "One day I'm going to be CEO of this company." Whitney added: "Dalton convinced Ward that if he picked anyone else, the company would ultimately crumble, because the entire top level of management would resign. He played Ward on that again and again until he had the CEO convinced that he would be left without anyone to manage the company."

Dalton's version was different. He later remembered having said when Ward offered him the job, "I'm not sure I want that job. I've been working since I was 18 and I've been planning to retire early so I can enjoy life a little more." Dalton also said that Ward, refusing to take "no" for an answer, replied, "I've trained you to be president and you'd better damn well take it or you'll be fired." Dalton accepted and became president in 1971 and CEO in 1973, while Ward remained chairman of the board.

5. To disguise the situation further we have not attributed comments to specific directors.

Whatever the truth in the differing recollections of Dalton
and Whitney, as events unfolded, an intense rivalry developed
between them, suggesting that Whitney may have wanted to
be Ward's successor. As tension between them built up at the
same time that Ward's and Dalton's relationship was deterio-
rating, the outside directors faced tension in the executive
suite, and in the boardroom, since the combatants were also
directors. (At the time, the company had 8 inside directors
and only 6 outsiders.)

Signs of Discord

The first signs of discord between Ward and Dalton began
soon after Dalton's promotion. According to Dalton:

> Charlie Ward resented the changes I initiated. He
> would go down two to three levels and, in effect, under-
> mine orders I'd personally issued. Sometimes he would
> do it directly and other times through innuendos, say-
> ing such things as "Bob doesn't know what he's doing
> throwing money into advertising; that's as good as
> throwing it down the drain. I don't think you should let
> him do that." It didn't take me long to realize that
> Ward was beginning to step on my toes.

As chairman, Ward maintained an office at the company's
headquarters and also chaired the executive committee, which
became involved in many operating decisions. His recollections differ considerably from Dalton's:

> [Dalton] exhibited a complete change of personality. He
> was the best bootlicker I ever saw until he got to power,
> and then he couldn't be vindictive enough against the
> people who had helped him along. Furthermore, he
> spent a great deal of time politicking with the board
> members. One of the first changes he made was in the
> pay of outside directors. I'd been paying them a total of
> $4,500 for meetings and everything. He quickly put
> them on a salary of $11,000 and more for every meeting
> they attended, so that they made as much as $20,000.
> He was buying the outside directors with the stockhold-
> ers' money. I must say, though, that it was very frustrat-

*ing to be in my position, because I have always be-
lieved that if you're going to give a man a job, you've
got to give him plenty of rope and let him either do
well or hang himself. Although there were things that
came along that I didn't agree with, I didn't object to
them.*

Although Ward interpreted the increased directors' fees
this way, in 1981, average fees for directors in similar-sized
companies were $19,000,[6] and Dalton indicated he was sim-
ply bringing his directors into line with their peers.

The retirement plan was another source of controversy
among the senior managers, since it had been invested in the
company's stock in the late 1960s, when the company was
growing rapidly. Therefore, the more highly paid long-service
employees with significant stockholdings wanted the freedom
to shift to other investments, when earnings began to decline.
In response, the board approved a plan allowing pension-plan
participants to do so, if they wished. Some inside directors did
reallocate their pension assets, because, according to Whitney:

*They no longer had confidence in the firm's future.
When I watched people who had been with the company for their entire careers losing confidence to the de-
gree that they would make the election to get out of
Harvest stock under the guise of diversification, I said,
"Whoa, I better get out too." I sold my personal holdings rather than my portion of the fund, though, because I didn't want to stir a confrontation. I knew full
well that as soon as Ward got hold of the stock sheet
and saw that I was selling my shares, he would say,
"Well, he doesn't have any confidence in me and therefore he can't be part of the team."*

Dalton and Whitney

At this point in our narrative, it is again difficult to judge
the accuracy of different accounts. For example, other executives contended that they shifted their pensions away from
Harvest stock, not because they had lost confidence in the

6. Jeremy Bacon, "Corporate Directorship Practices: Compensation, 1981" (New
   York: Research Report 815 from The Conference Board).

company, but because it seemed a prudent investment strategy. What is clear, however, is that friction existed not only
between Ward and Dalton, but also between Dalton and Whitney. The second rivalry became more evident as Dalton proposed major changes in marketing policies, changes that Whitney didn't support.

According to Whitney, Dalton was convinced that the
strategy changes were essential for the company's long-term
success, and he told Whitney that he didn't think the two
would ever be able to work out their differences. "I interpreted
those words as a signal to depart, so I put my keys on Dalton's
desk," Whitney said, "loaded up the contents of my office into
my station wagon, and drove away."

Again, Dalton's recollection differed. He remembered
feeling, in November 1980, that "the unrest between Whitney
and me made it very difficult for anyone at Harvest to perform
properly." He remembered contacting Ward at his beach home
in Maine to tell him he planned to let Whitney go. Despite
Ward's admonition, "Don't do anything until I get back, and
then we can hold an executive committee meeting," Dalton
went ahead and talked to Whitney, later claiming he had told
him, "If you don't stop taking opposite positions from me,
we'll have to part company." When Whitney suggested he
couldn't be fired, Dalton replied, "I'm sorry you said that,
because I'm the CEO of this corporation and, as far as I am
concerned, you can go get everything out of your desk by five
o'clock today. You've thrown down the gauntlet and, whether
you like it or not, you can only have one boss at a company
and that boss is me." Without his supporter, Ward, present,
Whitney had no recourse but to leave.

Immediately afterward, Dalton contacted all the outside
directors and explained what had occurred. According to Dalton, they all supported his action. He also got in touch with
the local newspaper and told reporters Whitney had "resigned
for personal reasons." Whitney, meanwhile, told Ward he was
no longer with Harvest. Both Ward and John Rizzo, retired
executive vice president of Harvest and Ward's closest ally,
urged Dalton to reconsider. Dalton insisted the decision was
irreversible, and the rift between the chairman and the CEO
widened.

When asked why he let Whitney go, Dalton replied, "Whitney is a brilliant guy who was an excellent marketing man, but about as mean and abrasive a person as you could ever hope to deal with." Furthermore, Dalton was convinced that Ward was "using Whitney as an information source from which to generate his criticism of me and the programs I was trying to initiate." In fact, since all marketing and sales personnel reported to Whitney, his dominance in this area was such that Dalton *would* have found it hard to change marketing practices without his support.

Declining Performance

The tension in the executive offices and the boardroom intensified because, as an outside director described the situation, "not only were factions forming on the board, but also the company wasn't making as much money." According to Whitney, who, at this juncture, watched from the sidelines, the decline was largely caused by Dalton's decision to change the marketing strategy: "[The plan] added overhead and changed lasts so drastically that, for example, the women's shoes no longer fit. The women's line, which at one time had been the most profitable, was all of a sudden running at a loss, as was the new boys'."

With declining performance, the company became an attractive takeover target. In early 1978, the CEO of a diversified consumer-products company visited Ward and Dalton to sound them out on a friendly takeover. Dalton's view was that "it wouldn't make much sense to have them buy us out with our own money, and I couldn't see an advantage to a merger for the stockholders. I told Charlie [Ward] how I felt, and he was furious. I think he wanted to sell for personal gains, since he owned 3% or 4% of the company stock."

Dalton pointed out that, in an effort to stop the tender offer, the board subsequently made Ward an offer, which he rejected, for his stock. Ward still favored selling the company, but for a different reason: "By that time, I was convinced that Dalton wasn't going to do the job that needed to be done. It was apparent to me that one of the first things a new owner was going to do was fire Bob Dalton, which was fine with me."

An outside director understood Ward's motivation: "Selling the company was the only way Charlie could have succeeded in firing Bob. The only problem was, the board wasn't really behind him."

An External Threat Rejected

In March 1980, a public tender offer was made for Harvest, forcing the directors to consider the bid. Ward called a board meeting, during which Harvest's investment bankers presented an extensive analysis of the $34-a-share bid. They concluded that the offering price was too low because, at that time, Harvest stock was selling at approximately $28 and, in liquidation, the shares would be worth closer to $46. Despite that, Ward wanted to continue the negotiations, rather than flatly refuse the offer. As he described it: "I'm not a believer in taking the first price on anything, and I felt sure that they would increase the offer. I was in a difficult position, because no matter what happened, Dalton didn't want to sell, because he saw it as a threat to his job and he had the board on his side."

At a meeting a week later, the board voted to reject the offer. Initially, Ward and his ally, Rizzo, apparently convinced that the potential acquirer would raise his offer, voted for acceptance. Once Ward understood that such negotiations would entail making a great deal of information public, he changed his vote, as did Rizzo, and the rejection was unanimous.

Turmoil in the Boardroom

The boardroom climate continued to deteriorate. According to an outside director: "The meetings were extremely unpleasant. Charlie Ward dominated most of the meetings, even though he wasn't the chief executive officer any longer."

Dalton's explanation was:

I tried to let him say everything he needed to say, because I thought it would be better just to let him release all of his venom so he would quiet down. During the board meetings he had the pulpit, so to speak, most of the time and he began speaking to the press regularly. He objected to everything, either rightly or wrongly.

Although Ward disrupted the meetings and the functioning of the board, the directors were in a quandary. According to two outside directors, Ward couldn't be fired by either the CEO or the board, because he was a representative of the shareholders, elected at the annual meeting. Dalton, for his part, still hoped to "convince Ward and Rizzo to contribute their expertise and knowledge because I believed that they were smart, that they had developed Harvest, and that they had helped me along."

Just before the 1980 annual meeting, the directors addressed the problem by voting, in a brief meeting, to eliminate the position of chairman. A contractual agreement was drafted, stating that Ward would retain his board position as elected representative of the shareholders, and that he would serve in an advisory capacity to management, but without a management position. Although the agreement was approved at the annual meeting, as well as by the board, the boardroom atmosphere worsened.

As tensions mounted, Dalton admits he spent more time on his feud with Ward than was wise.

> *I had so many meetings, both with board members and with other people in the company, that I didn't have as much time for company matters as I think I should have. Furthermore, the internal dissension was bound to have some influence on operations; it slowed things down, inhibited our people, and produced inaction.*

An outside director commented:

> *The company's performance was falling off at the time. I don't think it was because Bob was a bad operator; it's just that he couldn't very well have succeeded in running the company while fighting his battles with Charlie at the same time. He put so much effort and energy into defending himself, particularly in the press, that there is no way he could have done his job to the best of his abilities. Furthermore, the lack of*

harmony between the executives was not only causing damage to morale within the company, but was also weakening the value of its shares.

Because of the feud's adverse effects on both employees and financial performance, the board decided to omit Ward's and Rizzo's names from the slate of directors prepared for the February 1981 annual meeting. Thus, their terms simply expired.

After the annual meeting, however, Ward impugned Dalton's leadership in a press interview. His comments were so critical that the board appointed a special committee, consisting of four outside directors, "to assess the performance of the CEO as reflected in the operations of the company." The committee reported that Robert Dalton "at no time had exhibited any dereliction of duty, and therefore should be allowed to continue in office."

Subsequent Events

At the next board meeting, Dalton was elected chairman and, two years later, his successor was named CEO and chairman. Because of the depressed market price of the company's stock, Harvest was prey to both rumored and real share purchase by unfriendly "investors." Consequently, in 1984, the board sought and consummated a merger with a larger company, thus ending Harvest's existence as an independent company.

In Search of an Explanation

Questions remain in this sorry tale—was the outcome inevitable, and who was to blame? The participants, not surprisingly, have differing views. Several years later, Dalton called the situation "a classic case of the officers responding to their own ends, and to the short-term interests of the shareholders, rather than the long-term health of the company, and its employees, and shareholders."

Whitney faulted the board:

> *The board should have started raising critical question about the company's losses a lot sooner. They could have said, "Mr. Dalton, look here, you're going to*

have to do something. The domestic inventories are pil-
ing up and we're losing market share." This is where I
consider the board to have failed. I gave the board the
information on this decline annually, from 1977 to
1979, and the outside board members chose to ignore it.
It was all there in black and white, but they didn't dig
into it to determine what was really going on in the
company.

But Dalton contends there was a reason why the directors
didn't force the issue:

I don't think they really thought the impact was all
that severe, and part of the blame for that is mine. I
knew so much about what was going on in the com-
pany that, in my explanations to them, I probably
shortchanged them as far as giving the complete story
was concerned. I wonder whether or not I gave them
enough information to go ahead and take action. That
was my failure.

Here, Dalton points to a major impediment to board action
in a gradually building crisis. If the CEO doesn't recognize the
crisis and/or alert the board, it's hard for outside directors to
gauge the problems. But, as Dalton also pointed out, the majority of directors were insiders. If the CEO wasn't fully explaining the difficulties, it's unlikely that inside directors, his
subordinates, would do so. "They wouldn't really tell me
what they thought, because I was their boss," Dalton said. "I
was their leader and they believed in me, so I developed an
overconfidence in their support of me."

Ward commented: "Dalton had six votes [the insiders]*
that had to vote with him or else they'd be fired. They just did
whatever he wanted; it's hard for me to think of an instance
when they overruled him."

Other outside directors believed that Ward's decision to
remain as chairman was the critical variable. One commented:

If the company had had mandatory retirement at
65 and not put it in on Ward's sixty-fourth birthday but

---

* Excluding Ward and Rizzo.

> when he was 50, then it would have been a much
> smoother transition and none of this would have hap-
> pened. If Bob were a bad operator, it might have hap-
> pened anyway, but I don't think that he is.

Whitney agreed:

> Nobody could run the company with Ward around;
> he, unfortunately, just couldn't let go. It was his; he
> built it. In his opinion, he took nothing and made it
> into something, so he could do whatever he pleased. It
> made it very difficult for the management and it also
> made it very difficult for the outside board.

Of the four cases, this is the clearest example of a board's
inability to use its legal authority to resolve a crisis. Each
director had an explanation, and there is some truth in each.
However, at the heart of the problem lies the directors' close
relationship with management, especially the CEO, a circum-
stance that always makes gradual crises difficult to recognize
and resolve.

At Harvest, the situation was complicated by the two stars
in the drama being the current and past CEOs. Directors were
reluctant to act swiftly, because of their long and respectful
relationship with Ward, the man who had built the company
and had selected most of them to be on the board.

Similarly, they wanted to be helpful to Dalton. And as
Dalton himself points out, he may have unintentionally mis-
used his power by filtering information about the growing economic difficulties, making it harder for the directors to understand the significance of external trends.

Boardroom norms against open criticism of the CEO, or
outside contact among directors, added to the outside directors' failure to develop an independent understanding of management or a consensus to act. In our view, even though outsiders were a minority, had they united they could have forced
a different resolution.

Unlike Burlington Northern, where Davisson's approach
to Menk was the key to a successful resolution, Harvest had no
outside director who was willing or able to assert leadership.
Whether this was a matter of personality, or that no reasonable

director would have wanted to get in the middle of a three-way battle among Dalton, Ward, and Whitney, is left for the reader to decide. However, it is clear that the emergence of a leader from among the outside directors is essential to resolving such a crisis. Under the present system, such a development is left almost entirely to chance, with the hope that one or more directors will have the ability, conscience, time, and fortitude to take a leadership role.

Governing in Crisis

We don't suggest that these four cases represent all types of crises or conditions that directors may encounter. However, when added to the data from our interviews and questionnaire, they do lead to some generalizations that can help us understand the challenges directors confront when the fire alarm rings in the boardroom, and that may help directors when they face future crises, as well as persons concerned with improving corporate governance in these turbulent times.

We previously described the changes directors considered most significant as boards move from ordinary duties to crisis management. In analyzing our cases, we found that the nature of the crisis does affect the board's specific challenges, but we also learned something our interviews didn't reveal— the norms of delicate behavior and undiscussability carry over when a board struggles with crisis. While in three of the four cases, the directors overcame the barriers the norms created, at Burlington Northern the time it took to do so delayed resolution of the crisis. At Harvest, where the failure to recognize and/or act on the crisis lasted for years, the delay contributed to the company's demise.

The norms had a different impact at Martin Marietta and Dunntech, where they prevented directors from discussing fundamental premises and concerns. While those omissions didn't seem to affect the outcome adversely, one wonders how often the lack of truly open discussion *has* created problems. Thus, one generalization emerging from the cases is the importance of directors being aware of the norms and willing to

Figure 7-2

CHALLENGES OF CRISES

	Sudden	Gradual
External	Time Use of Experts Tension Among Accountabilities	Relationship with Management Information Board Leadership
Internal	Time Relationship with Management Board Leadership	Relationship with Management Information Board Leadership

deviate from them. If the norms are problematic in halycon times, they are more so in times of turmoil.

Another generalization is the existence of a pattern in the challenges facing directors, a pattern that varies according to the nature of the crisis, especially whether it is gradual or sudden (see Figure 7-2). A sudden, externally induced crisis places immense strains on directors' time, both personally, and in terms of pressure to act. As was particularly evident in the Martin Marietta case, the pressures inherent in such situations can exacerbate any conflicts that directors feel about their accountabilities. Some directors at Martin Marietta, for example, struggled over how to balance their concern for shareholders with their interest in the corporation's long-term future. The combination of conflicting views of accountability, intense time pressures, and norms of undiscussability militate against directors reaching a shared board purpose, and can hamper them in influencing critical and complicated decisions.

In a sudden, external crisis, directors also face the increased impact of outside experts who can use their knowledge to influence and constrain directors. Several directors at Martin Marietta, as well as many others, talked of how such crises had taught them the importance, *before* a crisis occurs, of defining, and setting limits on, the role they want the experts to play.

When the crisis is sudden but internal, time pressures can also create problems. Had the Dunntech directors, for example, chosen to be more involved in the succession question, time pressures would have been a greater issue for them. Several Dunntech directors did mention the importance of acting quickly to maintain employee morale. However, in sudden, internal crises, time pressures rank well below the central issue of reversing the normal power imbalance between management and the board to allow directors sufficient power to manage the crisis. The power imbalance complicates externally generated crises, too, when the management and the board, unlike at Martin Marietta, are in conflict. However, in sudden, internal crises, with management inevitably at the core of the problems, directors *must* alter the power imbalance if they are to resolve the situation. Thus, the emergence of a leader from among the directors becomes paramount in forging the consensus that will enable directors to use the power of the board's numerical superiority. Because this thorny issue is also a problem in gradual crises, we shall turn to a discussion of gradual crises.

In gradual crises, whether external or internal, we see the board's relationship with management as the key challenge. As illustrated at Burlington Northern, what begins as an external problem is often redefined by directors to be internal as well. Since directors define their job as selecting, appraising, rewarding, and, if necessary, replacing the CEO, the obvious way to resolve an external difficulty is to replace the CEO. At Harvest, where the key issue was also the board's relationship with management, the directors, unfortunately, never found the leadership to assert themselves.

In gradual crises, whether external or internal, the relationship between management and directors is more than just a matter of who's in charge, critical though that is. It also involves the fact that the basis of management's (the CEO's) normal power is information and knowledge, the lens through which directors are accustomed to viewing the company and its environment. As the CEO of Harvest pointed out, if the CEO fails to inform directors accurately, it's hard for the board to understand what's occurring, particularly for long-service directors, who are prone to develop the same emotional beliefs as managers, as was the case at Burlington Northern.

Thus, we believe that the most difficult crises are gradual ones, where directors must overcome their normal reticence and confront the CEO with responsibility for the problem. They must realize that the events that may have been going on for many years, indeed, add up to a crisis that requires dramatic action by the board. To gain real governing power, they must first understand, and then overcome their dependence on, the CEO. In any crisis where the board-CEO relationship must change, directors must find their own leadership. For most U.S. boards, where the chairman and CEO are one, if that individual is part of the problem, someone must step forward to lead his or her peers to a consensus, a unified group will, which is the real power by which directors can govern.

There is, however, no process to facilitate the emergence of a leader from the board and no certainty that one *will* emerge in a crisis. This vital ingredient of the board's ability to deal with crisis is largely left to chance. Given the high stakes involved for a company, its stakeholders, and for the economy as a whole, "chance" is both inadequate and unwise. We believe it is also unnecessary. With the wealth of talent in America's boardrooms, the wisdom to recognize, and the ability to resolve, crises already exists. In Chapter 8, we will suggest some steps to ensure that it is utilized.

Chapter 8

Increasing the Power to Govern

The Need for Change

The problems of American companies in global competition, the undervalued market price of equity shares, and the related wave of restructurings are, at least partially, attributable to failures of corporate governance. Not that directors fail to address crises eventually. As our cases illustrate, they usually do, but doing it often takes too long and sometimes happens too late. How beneficial it would be if part of a board's normal role was crisis prevention, and if its oversight ensured that neither the board nor management allowed the corporation to fall prey to gradually building crises, internal or external. Obviously, there is often no way to predict or prevent sudden crises. Moreover, despite recent trends toward more directors from outside, better information, and more board committees, directors often have difficulty performing their normal duties, let alone coping with crises.

In this chapter, we shall recapitulate the impediments to directors' capacity to govern effectively and the factors that enhance or constrain their real power (see Table 8-1), and present our suggestions for improvement.

Though the law gives directors the authority to manage the corporation's affairs, real power consists of more than legal authority. Group cohesion is their most significant additional

Table 8-1
Forces Affecting Directors' Power

Enhancing	Constraining
• Legal authority	• Limited time
• Group solidarity	• Limited knowledge and expertise
• Open style of CEOs	• Lack of consensus on goals
	• Group norms against:
	criticizing the CEO
	outside contact
	discussing accountability and other premises
	• Power of CEO
	knowledge and expertise
	control of agenda
	control of meetings
	control of information
	selection of directors

power source, as few CEOs can withstand the explicit consensus of a united board.

Outside directors, however, are seldom cohesive. These talented, successful individuals meet infrequently and relatively briefly at tightly structured meetings with a full agenda. Busy themselves, they don't object to the boardroom norm discouraging extrameeting contact. Add the norms that discourage open criticism of the CEO, and it's abundantly clear why directors find it hard to communicate freely with one another. Finally, boardroom norms against discussing fundamental premises and purposes, and the changing and complicated legal nature of director accountability to shareholders, who have little voice in director selection, and to other stakeholders, mean that directors are often unclear about their shared purpose.

But the most obvious impediment to outside directors exercising their power is that the acknowledged and formal leader in 80% of U.S. boardrooms is the CEO, whose power is greater, primarily because of his knowledge of and expertise in company matters. Although directors feel they receive adequate information, their time, knowledge, and interpretive ability are no match for those of a full-time and long-service CEO, and since the CEO determines what information directors receive, it's no exaggeration to say that, in most instances, directors understand the company through the CEO's eyes. In addition, the CEO controls the agenda, the meeting process, and, though less important on many boards, he or she still plays a key role in the selection of new outside directors.

In normal times and in crises, when the CEO and directors are united, the contradiction in legal and real power is managed in most boardrooms through a complicated social exchange, an arrangement reinforced by the fact that so many outside directors are also CEOs, who want to play by the golden rule. In exchange for directors' adherence to the norms, most CEOs develop a leadership style that permits board involvement and discussion and encourages directors to offer advice. When this arrangement is in place, many directors do have more influence and feel they make a contribution. Yet, in many boardrooms, fundamental problems and directors' concerns never surface, allowing small problems to become major ones before directors begin communicating with one another, understanding their collective problem, and acting. When the CEO is part of the problem, which he often is, especially in gradual crises, the difficulties are even greater. A loosely defined group, without an alternate leader, finds it difficult to take on the person who has been the real potentate in the boardroom, and a problem's resolution can take far too long. To return to the firefighting analogy, there is often a conflagration before the directors have gotten on the fire truck.

Perspectives on Changes

From our conclusions, we've developed specific recommendations about how boards of directors can become more like the potentates they are legally supposed to be. Because the problems are the result of a complex mixture of economic, financial, legal, organizational, and psychological forces, we realize readers will react differently to our proposals, particularly as those concerned with corporate governance have their own biases and perspectives.

Directors will wonder how our proposals will affect them in the boardroom, and whether they will enable them to govern more effectively. They may feel that some proposals push them too far over the line that has traditionally separated their duties from management's. Those who are also active CEOs may ask if the proposals will diminish their power on their own boards, further complicating an already difficult job. Those who are lawyers may be more concerned with the legal ramifications. We also know, from interviewing so many of them, that directors have varying degrees of concern about the need for change.

Readers who aren't directors but are interested in improving corporate governance will also have diverse reactions. Some representatives of institutional investors will be concerned about the impact of the ideas upon their gaining a stronger voice in selecting directors, for example. The legal fraternity, including judges, legislators, and regulators, may be vexed by our conclusions that legal authority alone is not sufficient and will be concerned with how the proposals relate to existing laws and regulations, and what changes those may require.

Given the complexity of the issues and the variety of viewpoints, it would be naive to believe that all readers will greet our ideas with equal enthusiasm, or that a particular reader will believe that all the proposals are desirable. Therefore, we divided our proposals into two categories: first, those that are essentially changes within the present legal and traditional system of corporate governance. In our view, these are the minimal changes needed to shift the balance of power between directors and management and are sufficiently modest to be acceptable to most CEOs and directors, while still having a rapid and positive impact. These innovations can be brought about by CEOs and directors in individual companies.

The second set of proposals, calling for broader, more complicated changes, is more controversial because it could dramatically alter the balance of power in America's boardrooms. While we respect the fact that many experienced CEOs and directors will find some of the latter ideas too radical, we believe these reforms are also needed if directors are truly to live up to their legal mandate. These changes would be difficult to implement, requiring changes in the laws of most states, in SEC regulations, in the rules of stock exchanges, as well as in the bylaws or charters of many corporations. Clearly this is an ambitious agenda and a complex, perhaps impossible, undertaking. If this study doesn't lead directly to such changes in the near term, we hope it will stimulate debate that will add momentum to attempts to improve American corporate governance.

Innovations within the System

Among the forces affecting directors' power (see Table 8-1), the most easily altered are those that limit the CEO's power in board matters, increase the power of the board's superior numbers through cohesion, and use the board's limited time more effectively.

Director Selection

Reducing CEO involvement would lessen directors' sense of obligation to the CEO and could be relatively easily achieved. Many boards already have nominating committees composed entirely of, and chaired by, outside directors, who consider the present composition of the board, anticipate retirements and other departures, then screen and select candidates for vacancies. We hope even more will adopt these practices. Realistically, the CEO would still influence the selection process, because a director unacceptable to the CEO would likely be ineffective.

Once the outside directors presented a list of possible candidates, the CEO, like any director, could suggest other potential candidates. After the nominating committee has identified a candidate, the CEO should have the opportunity to meet him or her, and to present an opinion to the nominating committee. In this way the nominating committee and its chairman would control the process and the final choices, yet the CEO would still have a voice. With such a change, new directors on all boards would clearly understand that they are selected by the nominating committee, on behalf of all directors and not just the CEO. No matter how directors are chosen, they're still subject to shareholder approval. Such elections are generally a formality, confirming the slate proposed by the incumbent directors, and within the present system, we see no practical means to change the situation.

Our concern with the heavy reliance on CEOs as outside directors is twofold. From a practical perspective, there aren't enough active CEOs to go around, if they continue to occupy 60% of outside board seats. Further, their preponderance and their natural CEO bias reinforce the dysfunctional boardroom norms we've noted, though we must view the objections in the context of arguments for so many CEO directors.

From the CEO's perspective, he or she gains invaluable knowledge as an outside director and may also have much to give, drawing on personal corporate experiences. However, since membership demands time commitments, being on too many boards could interfere with CEOs' capacity to lead their own companies. We suggest that, to guard against the unrestrained board joiner, nominating committees establish, as many do now, the number of boards on which a candidate can serve.

Those who select CEOs as directors believe their reasons are valid. A skeptic would argue that the CEOs generally prefer other CEOs because they'll be sympathetic and won't rock the boat. There may be some truth in the assertion but, more likely, CEOs and nominating committees believe that CEOs have the most relevant experience and expertise to be effective directors. CEOs understand the complex problems of running a major enterprise and, it is argued, provide the best counsel and advice. Since two major elements of the director's job are to assess top management and oversee strategy, there is, indeed, a logic in having directors who understand such issues.

Since there are too few active CEOs to meet the demand, one obvious solution is to rely more heavily on retired CEOs. In spite of one earlier study that found no correlation between directors' age and company performance, we believe using more retired CEOs has merit.[1] Older directors bring a breadth of experience and wisdom, both qualities essential for effec-

---

1. Phil L. Cochran, Steven L. Wartick, and Robert A. Wood, "The Average Age of Boards and Financial Performance," *Quarterly Journal of Business and Business Economics* (Autumn 1984), pp. 57–63. From our perspective, in spite of its serious intent, such a study is flawed in its design because there are so many variables that can or do impact on financial results than just the age of the directors.

tive corporate governance. Furthermore, increasing life expectancy and improved health in later life suggest that a CEO or other senior executive who steps down in his own company at 65 or earlier could serve perhaps 10 years as an outside director of another company. In addition, retired individuals, assuming they don't join too many boards, would have more time and attention to devote to their boards.

Boards that rely on older directors will also need a way to ensure that those who can no longer contribute step down. This problem is related to the broader question of who should, and how to, evaluate the performance of outside directors. Our own view is that effective evaluation of all directors is difficult to accomplish when a board is chaired by the CEO. Since the chairman is the logical person to perform director evaluations and the board's task is to assess the CEO's performance, asking CEO-chairmen to evaluate directors would further complicate the power imbalance. However, when directors' health or other abilities are in question, the nominating committee could well decide on a person's capacity to continue.

Another potential pool of experienced candidates is other top-level managers such as presidents, vice chairmen, and executive vice presidents. Whatever their title, they have had long experience in corporate management and, since still active, might bring a younger viewpoint to the boardroom. For these individuals and their companies, serving on a board or two could provide a valuable learning experience. A third pool of relevant talent is individuals who have occupied leadership roles in government, education, foundations, and medicine. Although they haven't led private companies, they are versed in the complexities of managing large institutions.

In making these suggestions, we are endorsing the prevailing viewpoint that leadership experience is important for a majority of directors. In fact, except for the heavy reliance on existing CEOs, the present composition of boards seems to provide an appropriate balance of experience and points of view. If those selected in the future are chosen in the manner described above, we believe they could come to the boardroom with a clearer recognition of their independence from the CEO and, therefore, with an enhanced sense of their power to govern.

Director Accountability

A second way to enhance directors' group power is to clarify the board's legal accountabilities. Currently many directors are trying to govern without a clear understanding of whose interests they are expected to uphold. There appear to be at least two reasons for their uncertainty. One is that legal responsibilities are changing because of new state laws and court decisions. Most directors are at best vaguely aware of the shifts and, since they don't discuss accountability among themselves, each director's definition of why, and in whose interests, he or she is governing is personal, and may differ from that of others. Because accountabilities are the fundamental premises upon which decisions are made, such confusion makes it difficult for the board to assert itself collectively and forcefully.

One solution is to have each company's legal counsel explicitly spell out directors' accountabilities, within the laws of the relevant state. Any confusion or lack of definition should also be made explicit. The directors should then discuss *their* understanding in order to reach a consensus or at least to be aware of the range of opinions. To the extent to which there is agreement, it would facilitate shared objectives and alleviate the conflict many directors presently feel between their own values and what they perceive to be their legal responsibilities. Agreement would not only enhance the board's capacity to govern, but would focus attention on the central purpose of corporate governance—the long-term viability of the company for all its stakeholders and for the nation.

Director Compensation

Linking some of their compensation directly to the company's long-term financial performance might encourage directors to focus on their broader responsibilities and to strengthen their resolve to govern in the long-term interests of the corporation and its several stakeholders. Such compensation might be in stock options tied to company performance, which would vest, for example, the fifth to ninth year out.[2]

2. The idea of stock options for directors was proposed by Myles Mace in "Stock Options for Outside Directors," *Harvard Business Review* (July–August 1977), p. 36. More recently, Walter J. Salmon has suggested this approach in a draft paper, "Public and Corporate Governance: Some Thoughts," December 1988.

Another possibility is an annual grant of a fixed number of shares (or a fixed dollar amount in shares) to directors, the idea being to enhance their long-term ownership position in the company. The shares or options might be in lieu of a percentage of cash fees, since current compensation levels seem satisfactory.

Because directors don't consider compensation and stock ownership an important reason for serving, we believe such proposals have merit for psychological reasons.[3] Although the stock accumulated wouldn't significantly add to their wealth, nor would they become major shareholders, it would increase their common identification with the corporation. Directors, like other successful individuals, are competitive—they like the feeling of winning. A stock incentive, or option plan, would play into these psychological needs by providing a yardstick by which to measure their success in governing the corporation. A feeling of success, along with a clearer understanding of accountability, would, we believe, give directors a stronger sense of shared purpose and, therefore, strengthen the collective power of each board.

Such incentives, added to the learning and challenge directors value, would strengthen the positive side of serving. In fact, from the legal traditional perspective, the major motivational factors, other than fees, are negative ones. At every juncture, a director risks being sued or publicly embarrassed, while the mere absence of legal entanglement or public embarrassment is the directors' reward for responsible conduct. This, we believe, is an additional argument for an incentive program to strengthen the directors' sense of purpose and their resolve to work actively together.

Two concerns, however, can be raised. One is philosophical, or legal: Would incentives reduce the distinction between the functions of directors versus those of employees? If their compensation were tied to corporate results, would directors be hindered in their role as overseers of management? We believe not, and suggest that a larger investment in the com-

---

3. In addition to our own data, Arch Patton and John C. Baker report in their study of boards of 74 companies that in 1985 only 11% of the directors owned more than 3,000 shares of the company's stock. "Why Directors Won't Rock the Boat," *Harvard Business Review* (November–December 1987), p. 11.

pany will, psychologically, increase feelings of ownership and foster a longer-term perspective.

A more practical concern is this: How should the system be structured to allocate the amount of such awards, without allowing—or tempting—directors to feather their own nests? Within the present system, the solution would seem to be a predetermined plan, subject to shareholder approval.

While there are ways to circumvent the most stringent safeguards, our suspicion is that few directors would do so, and even fewer boards would have enough rogues to permit abuses to proliferate. The only abuse we can envision would be an attempt to increase the short-term value of the company's stock. Under our proposals, there would be little financial incentive for directors to do so. Further, the mental set of most directors is so firmly focused on the long-term health of the corporation that we see little risk.

Director Activities

Effective time management. Time for both preparation and meetings is a major constraint on directors' capacity to govern. Given the caliber and busyness of directors, there is no realistic possibility that a director can or will devote more time to a particular board than he or she does now. More realistically, the problem is to make more efficient use of the available time. Greater reliance on committees is already a major step, but it's important to ascertain that directors are using their time to focus on three key tasks: selecting, advising, assessing, and replacing the CEO; strategic direction; and ensuring ethical, legal, and socially responsible conduct by managers and employees.

As long as the CEO controls the agenda, even the best-intentioned of them may inadvertently divert the board from its intended tasks. A desire to acquaint directors with younger managers, for example, can lead to lengthy presentations that curtail the time available for strategic issues; an overzealous corporate counsel can dwell too long on minor legal matters; or discussion of a series of relatively small capital expenditures can occupy a disproportionate amount of time. We believe there are ways to prevent such misallocations of time.

First, the CEO and directors should set an annual agenda for normal board activities. It might be a generic plan like the "wheel" at the Dayton-Hudson Corporation (see Figure 8-1), which outlines the board's major yearly duties. A broad plan such as this enables the CEO and directors to agree in advance on how and when various topics will be handled. The discussions should identify specific questions that the CEO, committee chairmen, or directors feel need discussing, so that all involved will know what the major agenda items will be, and how they relate to the board's principal duties. Such awareness should enable directors themselves to monitor the best use of time more effectively.

We urge any CEO or director who believes this kind of planning is not needed on his or her boards to audit how time is used at a series of typical meetings. We believe that review would reveal that many boards spend inordinate amounts of time on relatively unimportant matters—witness the Burlington Northern's review of land leases—that, because of their familiarity, go unnoticed.

Use of committees. The division of work between audit, compensation, and nominating committees and the full board, is usually clear. The committees delve into details the full board doesn't have time to consider and, as explained earlier, this process seems to work well. However, in strategic issues and matters pertaining to the CEO, the line between committee work and the full board's involvement becomes more controversial.

As we reported earlier, some directors worried that the expansion of strategic planning committees would preclude the full board from considering strategic questions. A similar issue arises about the cluster of CEO-related duties. In some companies, these matters are considered by the compensation committee.[4] Again, the concern is that the board will not be involved in the major issues directors consider to be theirs.

Our belief is that a strategic planning committee should create an agenda and frame the strategic issues for the full

---

4. Or a similar committee with a different name: for example, Organization and Management Committee or Personnel Committee.

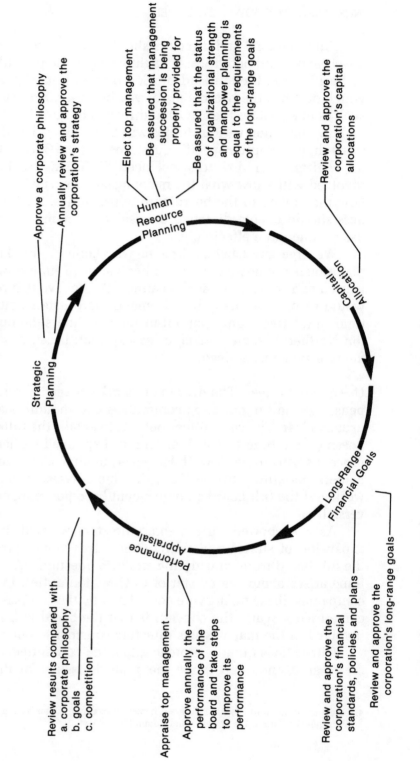

Figure 8-1

Dayton-Hudson Corporation

Board of Directors—Duties

Relationship to the Management Process

Approve a corporate philosophy

Annually review and approve the corporation's strategy

Elect top management

Be assured that management succession is being properly provided for

Be assured that the status of organizational strength and manpower planning is equal to the requirements of the long-range goals

Review and approve the corporation's capital allocations

Human Resource Planning

Strategic Planning

Capital Allocation

Long-Range Financial Goals

Performance Appraisal

Review results compared with
a. corporate philosophy
b. goals
c. competition

Appraise top management

Approve annually the performance of the board and take steps to improve its performance

Review and approve the corporation's financial standards, policies, and plans

Review and approve the corporation's long-range goals

board's discussion, but not prevent active board involvement in corporate strategy. For example, it should ensure that strategic discussions include consideration of how the company's businesses are performing and what businesses to be in, as well as an analysis of financial goals and capital structure, and its market value compared with its breakup value. The latter financial matters are emphasized, because the failure of some boards to be sufficiently cognizant of them has opened up opportunities for takeovers and LBOs.

Similarly, while no one challenges the efficacy of a committee to deal with routine compensation issues, and even to oversee normal management succession and human resource management questions, the board as a whole must be involved in matters concerning the CEO, because each director is engaged in an ongoing assessment of the CEO's performance, as he or she listens to the chief's report, considers company results, and assesses the quality of the managers who report to the CEO. For most directors, this is the most important task!

The Board's Activities

Assessing the CEO. In most boardrooms, directors have no legitimate forum in which to share judgments with one another or with the CEO. To remedy this problem, we believe every board should have a formal annual review of the CEO's performance, with sufficient time set aside and ways established for directors to discuss their assessment fully. Going beyond subjective impressions, the assessments should focus on how the CEO is performing in relation to the company's financial, strategic, and management-development goals. The data gathering and feedback to the CEO could be done by the chair of the compensation or personnel committee, by the committee as a whole, or in some other fashion.

We stress the importance of such evaluations for the CEO, and for the board. CEOs work in a world where critical feedback is rare, and almost never comes from inside directors or other subordinates. A formal review would give the CEO a balanced, full-board critique and enable directors to share their insights and concerns. It would also enable them, collectively, to recognize emerging problems more quickly. Directors who have to unseat a CEO will find the painful task less wrenching if, by forthright annual appraisals, they have done their best to alert the CEO to their misgivings. A meaningful review would also reinforce, in directors and signal management, the idea that the board intends to exercise fully its legal mandate to govern.

Using outside experts. At this point, our focus shifts from normal board activities to the importance of directors knowing in advance how, and to what extent, they want to utilize outside experts when a crisis occurs. Once a crisis arises, there may be no time for directors to consider the question.

First, directors need to understand their legal requirements to rely on outside authorities. Where does the expert advice end and where do directors' deliberations and decisions in closed sessions begin? Such understanding, like that of accountability, can be provided by an advance review of relevant state laws and court decisions, and discussions with the corporate counsel. Directors should also agree, in advance, about which outside experts to use. If during the course of a crisis there is need to change them or add new ones, there should also be agreed-upon procedures for doing so. Once directors have agreed how the experts will be selected and utilized and at what point they will be asked to withdraw, the board can consider their advice without being unduly influenced.

Boardroom Process

Modifying boardroom norms is critical to constructive change. As long as directors avoid discussing fundamental premises and goals, as long as they restrict criticism to pointed questions, and as long as they are unwilling to converse freely, in or out of meetings, with fellow directors, they will continue to dissipate the power of their numerical superiority. Open dialogue with one another and with the CEO is crucial for an ability to govern and, as we've documented, will allow directors to identify potential problems more quickly. Most important, greater cohesiveness will increase the real governing power of outside directors.

Clarifying accountability, planning the use of time, evaluating the CEO, and deciding how to use experts would encourage directors to discuss their goals openly and to express their opinions about CEO-and-company performance more candidly. However, there's a "Catch-22" in these recommendations because directors will find them hard to implement within prevailing boardroom norms.

One solution might be for us to implore directors who read this book to adopt the above suggestions. For example, they might compare boardroom discussions with productive sessions among managers or professionals in their home organizations, and modify their behavior accordingly. Unfortunately, such urgings may have little effect, because the norms are well established and endure because they enable CEOs and directors alike to manage the ambiguities of their relationships.

Change might come more readily if boards considered those norms as a group problem. There are established methods whereby groups examine their internal functioning with the help of process consultants, who identify dysfunctional norms and behaviors, the understanding of which leads to group commitments for change. Such efforts have improved the functioning of management decision-making groups at all organizational levels, and we believe that this kind of self-examination would help outside directors to work effectively as a group within the present governance system. They could learn to disagree with one another and the CEO without being disagreeable; and to challenge without being confrontational!

The Presiding Director

Other than planning how to use outside experts, our recommendations have focused on normal board activity. However, directors have the greatest difficulty under crisis conditions, especially when the CEO is incapacitated or is part of the problem. Even if we rule out radical changes in the present system, we believe directors need a way to organize themselves rapidly in a crisis. The present custom of waiting for "lightning to strike one director," or for rump sessions in hotel rooms and bars, relies on serendipity and can take too long.

We propose that, in advance, the outside directors elect

one of their number as presiding director, a contingent position, in which the incumbent would have no duties until the CEO was incapacitated, or a majority of outside directors felt the need for new board leadership. Under these conditions, the presiding director would call board meetings, set agendas, lead discussions to ameliorate the crisis, and, if necessary, call in outside experts. In essence, he or she would serve as chairman pro tem during the crisis.

Since a committee chairman, or the most senior director, might step forward in a crisis, some may feel this idea is unnecessary. Others will believe our proposal doesn't go far enough. For example, it could be argued that the presiding director should be actively involved at all times, working with the CEO to set agendas, appoint committee chairmen, and so on, but our idea of a presiding director is aimed at a specific purpose—to ensure that the board has a leader in crisis when the CEO cannot, or should not, play that role.

In fact, all of our proposals are modest and don't fundamentally alter the rules by which corporations are governed. Nor are they intended to challenge the CEO's role as corporate leader. Their intent is simply to enhance directors' power to govern. In developing these proposals, we have been mindful of our interviews and discussions with directors who themselves are active CEOs. We have tried to furnish a set of proposals that we believe improve the governance process without unduly infringing on the leadership role of the CEO.

Systemic Change

While these innovations *would* enhance directors' power, we believe more drastic ones are necessary, if directors are truly to fulfill their legal mandate. The changes we envisage would give directors greater real power and a clearer sense of purpose, connecting their own values to the vital role of corporations in American society.

A Separate Chairman

One major need is to diminish the CEO's power as leader of the board. To do this we suggest that, by law and by custom, the position of chairman and CEO be separated.⁵ Providing a leader separate from the CEO could significantly help directors prevent crises, as well as to act swiftly and effectively when one occurs. More generally, a separate chairman would give directors a strong voice in setting the agenda, in conducting meetings, and in selecting directors. He or she could be a constructive force in overcoming the dysfunctional norms of so many boardrooms, since a non-CEO board leader automatically eliminates much of the ambiguity in the director's relationship with the CEO. The chairman could also use control of the meeting process to encourage more open discussion. Finally, we believe that establishing such a position would send a clear signal to present and future directors and managers, reinforcing the board's right and obligation to govern, and reminding managers that it is they who serve at the pleasure of the directors.

As we mentioned, this is common in many United Kingdom companies, as well as in major nonprofit institutions, such as universities, hospitals, foundations, and museums in the United States. This arrangement obviously can and does work, though incumbent CEOs often argue that such a change would complicate their jobs. What they fail to add is that it would also weaken their power over their boards. Rather than dismiss those concerns as self-serving, it's important to recognize that some of the CEOs' worries do have merit.

One concern is that their predecessor would likely be appointed chairman. Such action could be easily avoided, however, if companies pass bylaw amendments prohibiting the former CEO from becoming chairman. Instead, outside directors could choose the chairman from among their number, a sound practice for two reasons. First, it's not in the corporation's best interest to have its retired CEO become chairman.

---

5. We are not alone in making this recommendation. In 1979 Harold Williams proposed this idea: "Corporate Accountability and Corporate Power," The 1979 Benjamin Farless Memorial Lectures, *Power and Accountability: The Changing Role of the Corporate Board* (Pittsburgh: Carnegie-Mellon University Press, 1979), p. 18. More recently, Patton and Baker have made the same proposal, "Why Directors Won't Rock the Boat," p. 12. See also Winthrop Knowlton and Ira Millstein, "Can the Board of Directors Help the American Corporation Earn the Immortality It Holds So Dear?" In *The U.S. Business Corporation: An Institution in Transition* (Cambridge, Mass.: Ballinger, 1988), pp. 169–191.

He or she might inhibit a successor from making necessary changes, because of personal objections, or because the new CEO was too sensitive to a predecessor's feelings.[6] Second, there is a benefit to making a clear distinction between the qualifications needed to be CEO and those of the chairman, since the latter would deal exclusively with board matters.[7] Selecting an outside director familiar with the company would also alleviate the fear that the chairman would lack the knowledge and information to be more than a parliamentarian.

Another issue for CEOs is how to define the two jobs. The British example is a useful model. The chairman, a nonexecutive, is responsible only for the smooth functioning of the board. In our view, this is appropriate for an American chairman as well. He or she would set the agenda, preside at board meetings, guide the process by which new directors are selected, determine committee membership and chairpersons, and ensure that directors are given adequate information. He or she would also play a central role in the board's evaluation of the CEO's performance. In fact, with a separate chairman, it would be feasible to consider a process for evaluating the performance of individual directors. While we have heard this idea discussed, we don't think it's practical unless the board leadership is separate from those the directors are governing. Clearly having a CEO-chairman evaluate the directors who are also evaluating him or her would only further complicate a problem-fraught relationship.

In order to carry out his or her responsibilities, the chairman would consult regularly with the CEO, whose job, except for an involvement in board matters, would not change markedly. The chairman's basic responsibility would still be to direct management operations, while the directors' responsibility would still be to oversee the process. Directors would continue to exercise their responsibilities, under the chairman's leadership, over the broad areas discussed in Chapter 4: assessment of top management, oversight of the formulation of

6. In fact, in our analysis of Harvest, we saw an example of the dangers of having an ex-CEO act as chairman.

7. Courtney Brown provides a useful description of a separate chairman's job: *Putting the Board to Work* (New York: Macmillan, 1976), pp. 41–50.

corporate strategy, compliance with the law, accounting principles, and ethical standards. Within these broad parameters, the CEO's job would still be to manage the company for the benefit of all its constituencies.

The advantages of having a separate chairman, rather than a presiding director, are clear. The chairman's position is operative in normal and crisis conditions, and his or her presence would counterbalance the CEO's power at all times. We believe both factors would enhance director power. The amount of time needed to be an effective chairman must, of course, be determined and would vary according to individual and company circumstances. The main considerations would be that the incumbent had time to do the job, and that his or her activities didn't interfere with the time and needs of the CEO to perform *his* or *her* duties.

Constituent Responsibilities

While there's still no visible movement in support of separating the positions of chairman and CEO, our second proposal—that directors be accountable to constituencies beyond the shareholders—is gaining support. Seventeen states have legislatively broadened directors' constituencies in their corporate laws, and judges are accepting the principle in rulings.

In addition, employee stock ownership plans (ESOPS) are growing in popularity because of favorable federal tax treatment, and a Delaware law stipulating that if employees own 15% or more of a company's stock, an acquirer must wait three years before consummating the deal. Such changes are further evidence of a trend recognizing the rights of employees as well as those of shareholders, and further legitimizing the directors' concern with broader constituencies.

We hope more states, especially Delaware, where so many major corporations are incorporated, will explicitly adopt broader constituency laws. There are two major arguments in favor of doing this. Most broadly, it would align the accountabilities of directors with the role of the corporation in our society. Corporations exist to provide more than a return to their owners—they also provide goods and services, and employment, which in turn produces taxpayers and contributes to the nation's economic well-being. Their conduct affects a wide range of national interests: the level of economic activity, the balance of payments, defense programs, technological innovation, charitable giving, and much more. It's no exaggeration to call them the heart of American society, more important to our national well-being than any other type of institution. If that is true, it makes no sense to instruct their governors to rule only for investors, especially now when so many investors are short-term institutional holders. While earning a return to shareholders is a fundamental tenet of our capitalist system, the emphasis on short-term values is inconsistent with the long-term viability of our economy. Choices have to be made between short- and long-term shareholder interests. Long-term corporate health also means considering other stakeholders. While it can be argued that paying attention to other institutions is beneficial to the shareholders over the long term, the cause-and-effect relationships are hard to establish. Making these kinds of judgment calls is a central facet of the director's job.

The second reason for proposing a wider accountability follows from the first. Although most CEOs and directors understand and agree with the logic of the argument, they still believe, often incorrectly, that they're accountable only to the shareholders. As we've said, this means that each director copes with the apparent inconsistency in a personal way. As a result, there is no explicit, shared understanding of the board's purpose to enable directors to have intelligent discussions and reach decisions about complex matters. Thus, we believe wider adoption of broad-constituency laws would reduce the ambiguity facing directors. In addition, the more clarity that can be brought to the laws of the 17 states already having such broad statutes, the better—whether it comes through legislative refinement or court decisions.

Director Selection

Earlier we made some modest proposals to diminish CEO influence on director selection. The creation of a separate chairman, however, would provide the ultimate assurance of that reduction, as it would be the chairman's job to ensure that the board membership was appropriate and that the nominating committee was finding the right people. The CEO's advice and counsel would still be sought because, as we noted, as the company's leader and as a director, his or her ideas about board composition must be considered. We believe, however, that the existence of a separate chairman and the changes outlined previously would put an end to the perception that directors are beholden to the CEO for their job.

We considered, and rejected, other possible changes in board composition. For example, several European countries, including Germany and the Netherlands, have labor representation on the board. We also considered the idea discussed by Senator Howard Metzenbaum and Ralph Nader in 1978, that there should be constituent representation on boards (that is, women, consumers, or minorities).[8] While recognizing the importance of the other stakeholders, we don't see how including them would contribute to the governance process. Many such representatives would be unlikely to have the breadth of experience a director needs. In addition, directors representing the viewpoint of one constituency or another could factionalize the board and impede decision making. This has happened in some European companies, and as a result some directors often discuss issues prior to formal meetings, to prevent a particular minority from easily blocking decisions. We also learned from interviews with union leaders serving on U.S. boards that their success stems from their identification, not only with their constituency, but with the well-being of all stakeholders.[9] In essence, with the exception of the heavy reliance on CEOs, the quality of the directors and the composition of the boards do not constitute a major problem of corporate governance.

The matter of constituent accountability also raises perhaps the thorniest question of all. Who should elect (or confirm) the directors, after incumbent directors select and nomi-

---

8. John Thackray, "America's Changing Boardrooms," *Management Today* (U.K.) (May 1978), pp. 58–61.

9. The most visible example of such representation was Lee Iacocca's ideas of recruiting Douglas Frazer, head of the United Auto Workers, for the Chrysler board.

nate them? The present system has several problems. First, since shareholders are offered only one slate, there are, essentially, no real elections, but we pointed out in Chapter 2 the impracticalities of creating more than one slate. Second, since there are so many institutional shareholders many of whose portfolios are constantly changing, it's often hard to identify them and their interests. While some advocate board seats for institutional investors, in our view this move could create a conflict between the fiduciary responsibilities to investors and the role as directors. Finally, if a director assumes that a board's role is only to satisfy the short-term investor, he or she is usually acting against his or her own conscience, as well as the long-term corporate and national interests.

There are no obvious means to ameliorate all these difficulties and simultaneously to provide directors with a clear, consistent message about their accountabilities. One idea we've heard is to permit only shareholders who have owned stock for a relatively long period, perhaps three years, to vote. While doing this would encourage directors to consider the shareholders' long-term interests, a drawback is the emphasis on shareholders, which ignores directors' obligations to other constituencies. Without becoming involved in the difficult and complex European system, we don't see any way to allow other stakeholders to "elect directors."

Another possibility is to legitimize what actually occurs by allowing incumbent directors legally to replace themselves. While such an act may seem radical, it would make the legal rules consistent with actual practice. If there were a separate chairman and the procedures outlined earlier about director selection were implemented, director choice would be independent of management. Again, there's a precedent for this suggestion in the nonprofit sector. At Harvard University, for example, such a process has selected the "directors" for over 350 years and it is used in many other universities, hospitals, and foundations. Of course, such an arrangement in the corporate arena would have to include a provision that, in the case of a change in control of company ownership, the new controlling interests could call for an election by the shareholders of a new slate of directors.

In considering this idea, it is natural to ask what checks

and balances ensure the directors won't run amok. One essential control, internal to the board itself, would be performance appraisal of each director by the chairman. Beyond this, in our judgment, the control over directors would rest exactly where it does today. First, any aggrieved party, especially shareholders, could bring legal action. Second, stockholders could vote with their feet. They could sell their shares and, of course, takeovers would still be possible and the new owners could change the board. Lenders could call in their loans. Customers could stop buying. Employees could quit, or strike. Any of the above actions, naturally, would lead to media attention and possible public embarrassment.

We aren't fully convinced of the superiority of this idea to others, such as allowing only longer-term shareholders to vote, or giving seats to large institutional holders. Rather, we put it forward for consideration. Our hope is that our ideas, plus new ones, will provoke a vigorous debate about how, or whether, directors should be elected after they are nominated. What seems vital is to create a process that isn't a legal fiction, and that enhances the legitimacy of directors' power to govern.

Time to Govern

Finally, we want to discuss how to give directors more time to do their jobs. As we've seen, directors are people with limited time, and, in many companies, the inertia of tradition rather than a careful analysis of the amount of time directors need to handle their work dictates the number, and length, of board meetings.

We hope that directors after careful analysis will establish how much time they need to be effective, and how to utilize their meeting time more efficiently. For example, it may well be that for companies with most directors located far from headquarters, fewer but longer meetings would be a more efficient use of directors' limited time.

Others have suggested fundamental changes to solve the directors' time constraints. For example, Patton and Baker recommended limiting the number of boards on which an active CEO could serve.[10] While we agree with the intent of such

10. Patton and Baker, "Why Directors Won't Rock the Boat," p. 12.

proposals, we believe it's impractical to set a definitive limit. Individual circumstances, and the time requirements of different boards, vary too much to establish rigid rules. A more flexible solution would require by law that directors stipulate, before joining, that they will have adequate time to serve. This agreement could take the form of a letter between each director and the chairman, in which the company would specify the director's duties, the time required, and the compensation to be paid, while the director would stipulate his or her understanding of these conditions and willingness and ability to meet them. This procedure wouldn't solve all time problems, but it would force individual directors to consider carefully the issue of time just as they now must consider potential conflicts of interest.

The Director's Job

In order to govern, outside directors must have the time, information, and power to assess a CEO's performance in all its aspects, to reward as well as sanction when performance falters, and to make a change if one is deemed necessary. The CEO's job includes both guiding and implementing the strategic direction of the company, as well as developing the next generation of management. The director's is to ensure that he or she does it well in an ethical manner and within the law. All our proposals, whether modest or more radical, are intended to enhance the director's power to perform his or her job well.

To do so, directors must have the ability to assess and influence the long-term strategic direction of the company, and to understand and evaluate the quality of management moving toward the top. These are the essentials of a director's job under normal circumstances. If directors do it well, we believe that many of the crises that have stricken so many companies will be avoided.

Directors must not wait passively for a crisis before they intervene. Their job, even in the normal course of events, is an important one, and they must have the necessary power to do it. Power, as we have used the term, implies the time and knowledge, which not only contribute to power but also allow its intelligent applications.

Some of America's foremost talents are devoting themselves to corporate governance. They are serving because directorship is an exciting, challenging job. If there is agreement that the job is important and that, typically, the right individuals are in position, then they should be given the tools to do the job. The purpose of this book has been to describe the tools they need, and our concluding chapter provides a metaphorical tool chest. But there is a difference between how our tools should be applied and the way real tools are used. A craftsman selects a particular tool for a specific job. Those who can make the changes that will empower directors truly to govern—legislators, judges, regulators, CEOs, and directors themselves—will need many tools simultaneously if they are to change the existing balance of power, and they will need the skill of a master craftsman as they carefully carve a new corporate reality.

It is our hope that the analyses and ideas in this book will contribute to changes already underway, to make directors more like the corporate potentates the law intends them to be than the management pawns they have too often been in the past.

Index

195